PENGUIN CLASSICS

THE MAN WHO HAD ALL THE LUCK

ARTHUR MILLER was born in New York City in 1915 and studied at the University of Michigan. His plays include *All My Sons*
(1947), *Death of a Salesman* (1949), *The Crucible* (1953), *A
View from the Bridge* and *A Memory of Two Mondays* (1955),
After the Fall (1964), *Incident at Vichy* (1965), *The Price* (1968),
The Creation of the World and Other Business (1972), and *The
American Clock* (1980). He has also written two novels, *Focus*
(1945) and *The Misfits,* which was filmed in 1960, and the text
for *In Russia* (1969), *In the Country* (1977), and *Chinese En-
counters* (1979), three books of photographs by Inge Morath. His
most recent works include a memoir, *Timebends* (1987), the plays
The Ride Down Mt. Morgan (1991), *The Last Yankee* (1993),
Broken Glass (1994), and *Mr. Peters' Connections* (1999), *Echoes
Down the Corridor: Collected Essays, 1944–2000,* and *On Politics and the Art of Acting* (2001). He has twice won the New
York Drama Critics Circle Award, and in 1949 he was awarded
the Pulitzer Prize.

CHRISTOPHER BIGSBY has published more than twenty-five books
on British and American culture. His works include studies of
African-American writing, American theater, English drama, and
popular culture. He is the author of four novels, *Hester, Pearl,
Still Lives,* and *Beautiful Dreamer,* and he has written plays for
radio and television. He is also a regular broadcaster for the BBC.
He is currently professor of American Studies at the University of
East Anglia, in Norwich, England.

BY ARTHUR MILLER

DRAMA
The Golden Years
The Man Who Had All the Luck
All My Sons
Death of a Salesman
An Enemy of the People (*adaptation of the play by Ibsen*)
The Crucible
A View from the Bridge
After the Fall
Incident at Vichy
The Price
The American Clock
The Creation of the World and Other Business
The Archbishop's Ceiling
The Ride Down Mt. Morgan
Broken Glass
Mr. Peters' Connections

ONE-ACT PLAYS
A View from the Bridge, *one-act version, with* A Memory of Two Mondays
Elegy for a Lady (*in* Two-Way Mirror)
Some Kind of Love Story (*in* Two-Way Mirror)
I Can't Remember Anything (*in* Danger: Memory!)
Clara (*in* Danger: Memory!)
The Last Yankee

OTHER WORKS
Situation Normal
The Misfits (*a cinema novel*)
Focus (*a novel*)
I Don't Need You Anymore (*short stories*)
In the Country (*reportage with Inge Morath photographs*)
Chinese Encounters (*reportage with Inge Morath photographs*)
In Russia (*reportage with Inge Morath photographs*)
Salesman in Beijing (*a memoir*)
Timebends (*autobiography*)
Homely Girl, A Life (*novella*)
On Politics and the Art of Acting

COLLECTIONS
Arthur Miller's Collected Plays (Volumes I and II)
The Portable Arthur Miller
The Theater Essays of Arthur Miller (*Robert Martin, editor*)
Echoes Down the Corridor: Collected Essays, 1944–2000

VIKING CRITICAL LIBRARY EDITIONS
Death of a Salesman (*edited by Gerald Weales*)
The Crucible (*edited by Gerald Weales*)

TELEVISION WORKS
Playing for Time

SCREENPLAYS
The Misfits
Everybody Wins
The Crucible

ARTHUR MILLER

The Man Who Had
All the Luck

A FABLE

Introduction by
CHRISTOPHER BIGSBY

PENGUIN BOOKS

PENGUIN BOOKS

Published by the Penguin Group

Penguin Group (USA) Inc., 375 Hudson Street, New York, New York 10014, U.S.A.

Penguin Books Ltd, 80 Strand, London WC2R 0RL, England

Penguin Books Australia Ltd, 250 Camberwell Road, Camberwell, Victoria 3124, Australia

Penguin Books Canada Ltd, 10 Alcorn Avenue, Toronto, Ontario, Canada M4V 3B2

Penguin Books India (P) Ltd, 11 Community Centre, Panchsheel Park, New Delhi – 110 017, India

Penguin Group (NZ), Cnr Airborne and Rosedale Roads, Albany, Auckland 1310, New Zealand

Penguin Books (South Africa) (Pty) Ltd, 24 Sturdee Avenue, Rosebank, Johannesburg 2196, South Africa

Penguin Books Ltd, Registered Offices: 80 Strand, London WC2R 0RL, England

First published in Great Britain in a volume with *The Golden Years* by Methuen Books 1989
This edition with an introduction by Christopher Bigsby published in Penguin Books 2004

1 3 5 7 9 10 8 6 4 2

Copyright © Arthur Miller, 1989
Introduction copyright © Christopher Bigsby, 2004
All rights reserved

LIBRARY OF CONGRESS CATALOGING IN PUBLICATION DATA

Miller, Arthur, 1915–
The man who had all the luck : a drama in three acts / Artur Miller ; with
an introduction by Christopher Bigsby.
p.   cm.
Includes bibliographical references (p.).
ISBN 0-14-243786-7
1. Alienation (Social psychology)—Drama   2. Failure (Psychology)—Drama
3. Success in business—Drama   I. Title.

PS3525.I5156M36 2004
812'.52—dc22   2003068909

Printed in the United States of America
Set in Sabon

Contents

Introduction

In 1938, Arthur Miller left the University of Michigan, at Ann Arbor, with high hopes. He had twice won the prestigious Hopwood Award for drama and once been runner-up. One of his plays had even been staged, albeit for a single night, by the Federal Theatre in Detroit. He returned to New York confident that he could conquer Broadway. After all, the Hopwood judges had been drawn from the New York theatre world and he did quickly join the Federal Theatre, an invention of FDR's Works Progress Administration.

Even as he tried to sell one of his Michigan plays, revising it in the basement of his family's Brooklyn home, he was writing another—the story of Montezuma and Cortez—perfect for the large casts that the Federal Theatre could afford. Despite encouraging words from his agent, from producers, actors and fellow writers, however, nothing happened, and in 1939 the Federal Theatre was closed down, suspected of Communist subversion. Broadway, meanwhile, showed no interest.

The theatre, though, was only one possibility and if it proved resistant there were always short stories or the novel. He wrote both but failed to place them. The only market he succeeded in penetrating was that for radio drama, though this in itself opened up other possibilities. He worked, briefly, for the Library of Congress and was also commissioned to write the screenplay for a film inspired, in part, by the dispatches of war correspondent Ernie Pyle. This took him to military bases around the country and though the final film—*The Story of GI Joe*—was written by others, in 1944 he published a book about his experiences: *Situation Normal*.

These ventures were financially rewarding but scarcely satis-
fying for a man whose eyes were still on Broadway. Then came
his breakthrough. A play he had originally written as a novel
was accepted. At twenty-nine, and after six years, he had,
seemingly, arrived. He was to be produced on Broadway, today, of course, a virtual impossibility for a first-time writer. The
play, *The Man Who Had All the Luck,* was to star Karl Swen-
son, who had appeared in several of Miller's radio plays. Its
out-of-town tryout was in Wilmington, its premiere at the For-
rest Theatre in New York on November 23, 1944. It should
have been a triumph; instead it was a disaster. Luck, it seemed,
was in short supply.

Both novel and then play were inspired by a story he had
originally heard from his wife's mother. She told of a relative
who had hanged himself from a rafter in his Ohio barn. What
intrigued Miller, and bewildered the man's wife, was that he
had been popular, never wanting for a job even in the middle of
the Depression. Then he developed what was plainly a mental
disorder. By then the owner of a filling station, one of several
properties he acquired while still in his twenties, he had begun
obsessively to check the books, afraid of embezzlement by his
staff. The paranoia grew and, despite treatment, he killed himself. What interested Miller was not his psychosis but the no-
tion of a successful man being drawn toward death, more
especially in a rural setting, away from urban pressures.

He was intrigued not least because his cousin's husband,
Moe, had also died suddenly. Another successful man, he, too,
prospered even during the Depression when others were fail-
ing. Going for a swim at Brighton Beach, he had collapsed, his
body, bizarrely, driven back to his home by the doctor who had
tried in vain to revive him. The arbitrary seemed at work both
in his rise and his fall.

If he had seemingly been chosen for preferment, he was just
as capriciously transformed into cosmic victim, born, it seemed,
with no greater purpose than to die. *The Man Who Had All the
Luck,* at least in its first form, was thus an exploration of the
absurd, of the fact that, as a Beckett character would observe,
humankind gives birth astride of a grave. By reversing the po-

larity and staging the plight of the man seemingly immune to disaster—a man who has all the luck—Miller explores, by inference, the implications of the man for whom disaster is an unearned fate, indeed of mankind for whom it is arguably likewise.

This is a dark fable reminiscent in certain respects of Camus's 1938 play *Caligula,* as the central character tests the proposition that there is no governing principle to existence, no inherent meaning, while desperately hoping for evidence to the contrary.

The Man Who Had All the Luck, in its various versions, "wrestled," Miller explained, with the unanswerable—the question of the justice of fate, how it was that one man failed and another, no less capable, achieved some glory in life. Miller later speculated that his interest might have been fired by his sense of his own talents and success and the contrasting lack of them in others. Also, kept out of war as a result of a football injury, he was aware that he flourished where others, including his own brother, risked death on a daily basis. For them, life was suspended and even forfeit; for him it offered opportunity, a family life and, if as yet only to a modest degree, success. Where was the justice in that? Was there some underlying moral order in the world or was everything the product of mere chance? And if the latter, could that be the basis for anything but despair?

The novel, which preceded the play, concerns David, a young man in his twenties, talented and successful, in everything he does. Setting himself up as a mechanic, he manages to get by on instinct until confronted with a car whose fault he cannot diagnose. He takes it to a specialist garage in a neighboring town but accepts the credit for the repairs they effect. As a result his reputation as a mechanic is enhanced and he secures a contract to work on the tractors of a neighboring farmer. From there his business grows. Slowly he adds other ventures, in which he is equally successful. But he is increasingly aware that he is surrounded by those who have failed in life, as he is of the lie on which his own career had been constructed.

One friend, Shory, had lost his legs during the war and as a result feels unworthy of the woman he loves. Another, Amos, was trained by his father to be a baseball pitcher but, despite his talent, fails to be taken on by the major leagues because his training, directed by his father in the basement of their house, has made him insensitive to other aspects of the game. A third friend, J.B. Fellers, appears to thrive, even having the child that he and his wife had desperately wanted, only inadvertently to kill that child when drunk.

For David, by contrast, everything goes well. He has the child he wanted and succeeds in everything he tries; but his very success breeds a deepening paranoia. He awaits the catastrophe he feels must balance his luck, if there is to be true justice in the world. He begins, like the man on whom he was in part modeled, to inspect the books of the gas station he owns. He prepares himself for what he feels must be the death of his own child, in some kind of perverted trade-off for a life otherwise without blemish. And, finally, he commits suicide, vaguely feeling that he will thereby lift the curse that surely must be on his family.

Perhaps that death is a sign that the novel was still too close to its origins, but perhaps it is also evidence of the fact that, to Miller, death raised the stakes, gave a deepening significance. He was reaching for the tragic but being snared by the merely pathological. When he came to write the play version he chose a different ending. He also introduced a number of changes, at least one of which would prove of lasting significance.

The play finds David Beeves's marriage to Hester blocked by her father. A bitter and cynical man, he is abruptly killed off in a traffic accident. The first obstacle to success is thus conveniently removed, that very convenience being a clue to the style of a play that Miller chooses to call "A Fable." Its very improbabilities (David buys a gas station, and a highway development fortuitously makes it profitable; he invests in mink, and survives an accident that wipes out a rival's holdings) are indicators of its status as a moral tale and, indeed, it was the inability of the director to define a style appropriate to this that in part accounted for its initial failure.

When David is confronted with a fault in a car that defies his skills, he is saved not, as in the novel, by taking it to another garage but by the arrival of an Austrian mechanic called Gus.

Two elements of the novel are thus tied together while the second obstacle to David's success is removed. And so he emerges as the man who had all the luck, in contrast to those around him, though the subplots that had overloaded the novel are now pared back. Meanwhile, the would-be young baseball player is integrated into the story when Miller makes him David's brother, a crucial change not only for this play but for his future work.

As he later explained, "*The Man Who Had All the Luck,* through its endless versions, was to move me inch by inch toward my first open awareness of father-son and brother-brother conflict. . . . One day, quite suddenly, I saw that Amos and David were brothers and Pat their father. There was a different anguish in the story now, an indescribable new certainty that I could speak from deep within myself, had seen something no one else had ever seen."[1] Only now recognizing that two of his university plays had also featured brothers, Miller, who was himself one of two brothers, felt he understood something of the tension that underlay the play.

Father/son relationships, those between brothers, suddenly opened up new possibilities that Miller would deploy in his work for another two decades and more. Within the family unit, he came to feel, are contained alternative possibilities, tensions that are, in some senses, the fragmented parts of a self (spiritual/material, poetic/prosaic, blessed/cursed). The evidence for that seems clear in *Death of a Salesman* and *The Price,* where the brothers have a dialectical relationship to one another, albeit one suffused with ambiguities. Father/son relationships, meanwhile, bring past and present together, hopes and fulfillments, or otherwise. They are the locus of anxieties about identity, of contested values, of an ambivalent love, of guilt. In the context of *The Man Who Had All the Luck,* though, Miller's decision to make David and Amos brothers seems primarily to have rooted the piece in a psychology he could understand and inhabit.

At the heart of the play is a concern with the extent of human freedom. Beyond offering an account of a man's decline into madness, and eventual redemption, it explores the degree to which so many of the characters become complicit in their own irrelevance, the extent to which they collude in the idea of man as victim, a mere object of cosmic ironies. At its center is the existential conviction, resisted by most of the characters, including David in his madness, that we are the sum of our actions. If not believers in God, a number of them are believers in fate, which is the word they choose to give to their own personal and social paralysis. For them chance *is* the operative principle in life and if that is so it is illusory to believe that one can deflect one's fate. Destiny is an excuse for inaction. Identity is a product of contingency. A Darwinian logic, selecting in favor of some and against others, appears the only observable principle.

As the play develops, David himself is a convert to this faith. He looks for some justice, some sense of social and perhaps even metaphysical coherence in existence. Finding none, he comes close to destroying himself, sure now that he has no power or reason to intervene in his own life, as if his suicide might constitute that balancing justice whose absence has brought him close to despair.

It is not hard to see how Miller regarded this as in some ways addressing that political and moral paralysis that he saw infecting Europeans and Americans alike in the face of fascism. To him, such inaction revealed something more than a failure of will, something beyond mere political pragmatism. It was as if belief in the possibility of action had been destroyed, as if the march of fascism across Europe were a natural and hence irresistible phenomenon. Beyond that, he seems to have detected a more fundamental defeatism, since this is a novel and then a play in which characters, acknowledging what seems to them to be the sheer arbitrary nature of experience, appear to accept the role of victim, to welcome the sense of vertigo that comes with staring into the depths of a self-generated despair.

For David, this was not always so. At the beginning of the play he is a man who seizes the day. In the words of his brother, Amos, he knows "how to do." Others are more quiescent. Thus his father wants success for Amos, having trained him for years, but it is David who finally calls the baseball scout, asking, "Can you *just wait for something to happen*?" By contrast, Shory, in part an echo of the figure of Moe Axelrod in Clifford Odets's *Awake and Sing,* has been made cynical by his wartime experience. For him, "A man is a jellyfish. The tide goes in and the tide goes out. About what happens to him, a man has very little say." Gus, the Austrian mechanic, likewise initially insists that "there is no justice in this world."

This is a view that David at first resists, if only because not to resist it would bring him to the brink of madness. As he says, "If one way or another a man don't receive according to what he deserves inside . . . well, it's a madhouse." Yet this principle seems not to be operative. Many of those around him fail, and as evidence of this accumulates he feels a rising tide of hopelessness and a despair that transmutes into madness. He can take no pleasure in a success that he feels no less arbitrary than the failure of those others. He becomes increasingly desperate. Like Willy Loman, he buys a life insurance policy as though the balance he looks for could be secured by trading his life for the future of his family. It is a bargain whose irony escapes him.

Whom, after all, is he bargaining with except the God for whose existence he can find no convincing evidence? If we do not exist in God's eye, then what is our sanction to exist at all? If God does not exist, then all things are possible. It was a question that fascinated both Sartre and Camus and that also concerned Miller, if not his Broadway audience or, perhaps more accurately, the critics who were Broadway's gatekeepers. There is a world of difference between Miller's protagonist and Camus's Caligula, but both of them test out the absurdist proposition that there is not only no moral sanction but no moral system at all. In the novel David goes to his death, a victim of his own belief in the absurd. In the play he learns a social ethic born out of a private understanding of agency.

David's identity and social role, then, are initially invested in the idea that he is literally the maker of his own future: but as doubts begin to intrude, that meaning starts to dissolve. The focus shifts to his deepening anxieties. His state of mind begins to determine the shape if not of events then of his perception of them. The play, in effect, takes an inward track as David filters experience for its meaning, or, increasingly, its perceived lack of meaning. His life, and what he chooses to make of the lives of those around him, is less lived than shaped by himself into an exemplary tale. He stands outside himself, watching, as if powerless to act.

He is alienated from his life because he cannot identify the transcendent purpose that he believes alone can charge it with significance. His identity comes close to being destroyed because he chooses to see it in terms of that absent force. Balanced between hope and despair, he fails, for much of the play, to recognize the truth that he holds his own life in his hands and that there are connections—those with wife, child, friends—that contain the essence of the very meaning he has sought in an abstract principle. In this he is close kin to Willy Loman, in *Death of a Salesman,* who would be dazzled by a dream that blinds him to those who value him for himself.

It is Gus who explains what David has lost, in doing so making the most explicit reference to the wider issues involved: "What a man must have, what a man must believe. That on this earth he is the boss of his own life. Not the leafs in the teacups, not the stars. In Europe I seen already millions of Davids walking around, millions. They gave up to know . . . that they deserve this world." Man, he explains, is his own God and "must understand the presence of God in his hands."

In the novel David dies; in the play he lives. He does so because he is finally convinced that his success has indeed been a product of his own hands, just as the failure of some of those around him can be traced to their own culpability. Shory, it turns out, bore responsibility for the loss of his legs which occurred not on the battlefront but in an accident at a whorehouse. J.B.'s life has never been what he hoped because of his drinking, though in this version he does not suffer the loss of his child. Amos and his father have narrowed their lives down until they have lost sight of what living might be. Such lives are still in part the product of contingency, but that contingency is not definitional. The thunder, representing arbitrariness, rumbles but, despite his apprehension, David calls out the central existential truth: "I'm here!"

Writing later, Miller remarked that "the play's action seemed to demand David's tragic death, but that was intolerable to my rationalist viewpoint. In the early forties," he added, "such an ending would have seemed to be obscurantist."[2] But the point was that in the novel it *had* ended with David's death. It was a death, however, that seemed to owe rather more to melodrama than tragedy, and in the play version Miller was stepping back from melodrama and tragedy alike. For him,

> A play's action, much like an individual's acts, is more revealing than its speeches, and this play embodied a desperate quest on David's part for an authentication of his identity, a longing for a break in the cosmic silence that alone would bestow a faith in life itself. To put it another way, David has succeeded in piling up treasures that rust, from which his spirit has already fled; it was a paradox that would weave through every play that followed.[3]

That last remark is especially interesting, both in its stress on the absences felt so acutely by his characters and in the biblical language. Miller recounts a conversation with John Anderson, critic for the *Journal-American,* who asked him, in the context of this play, whether he was religious. At the time he found the question absurd, yet of course the play in many ways focuses on the protagonist's fear of abandonment, his sense that some coherent principle is in abeyance. David wishes to invent the God in whom, on one level, he does not believe in order to discover justification, explanation, a sense of justice for which he can otherwise find no evidence. He resists the truth, which is resisted by so many of Miller's later protagonists, that he is his own connection, his own god, fully responsible for who he is and what he does.

The director Paul Unwin's response to the stylistic problems raised by the play, in the Bristol Old Vic production in England fifty years later, was in part to turn to music, specially composed by Andy Sheppard, and in part to rely on the designs of Sally Crabb, whose productions had included *The Master Builder* and *Our Town,* two plays whose style also moves away from realism and which, in effect, also offer themselves as fables.

In talking to Unwin before the production Miller observed that "the thing you've got to understand about my plays is that the background is the American dream and the foreground the American nightmare."[4] And, in one way or another, the characters in *The Man Who Had All the Luck* are dedicated to a dream while the process of the play is to move from dream to nightmare, precisely the transition that offers such a challenge to directors, actors and designers. Meanwhile, like Susan Glaspell's *The Verge,* it also has to move from the comic not to the tragic but, briefly, to the psychotic.

David is the paradigm of that dream, beginning with nothing and rising to success and wealth, the "treasures that rust, from which his spirit has already fled." He is even, in Willy Loman's term, well-liked, before, like Willy, though for wholly different reasons, developing a fevered need to justify his own existence. For Willy, the problem is failure; for David, it is success. He is, indeed, a mirror image of Job, who was stripped of everything in a test of his faith. David is given everything in a test of his. It is not the fallacy, or otherwise, of the dream, though, that compels Miller's attention here, nor primarily its social implications. Despite his remarks, the play is not a critique of the American dream, except insofar as David looks for meaning in the wrong place. What it is, in essence, is a debate about the source and nature of meaning in private and public life alike.

David feels the need to argue for the existence of God, or imminent justice, on the grounds that without such a concept, without a principle of order in the universe, nothing can have meaning. When, as it seems, sheer chance becomes the only observable mechanism at work in his own life and in that of those around him, he is terrified. The idea that things simply happen is intolerable. As far as he can see, some succeed and others fail and there is no reason for it.

In the play, as opposed to the novel, David emerges from his trial of the spirit, not yet secure, to be sure, but seemingly convinced that the logic for which he had looked does exist. People, he comes finally to believe, are responsible for their actions;

causality is an operative principle. But the wound is not entirely healed. The thought that "anything can happen ... at any time" is not purged and the desperate desire for a validating reason not entirely answered by acknowledging his responsibility for his own actions. The arbitrary still exists and, indeed, in invoking the Depression as a presence in the play Miller was doing no more than signal a social, economic and psychological truth of the period.

The collapse of the market was like one of Job's plagues. People lost livelihoods, relationships were attenuated, the future itself seemed suddenly to collapse. And if some people prospered, how much deeper the irony generated by that fact. Miller himself has said, "Until 1929 I thought things were pretty solid. Specifically, I thought—like most Americans—that somebody was in charge. I didn't know who it was, but it was probably a businessman, and he was a realist, a no-nonsense fellow, practical, honest, responsible. In 1929 he jumped out of a window. It was bewildering."[5]

The Depression was an economic fact but its consequences went beyond social effects. A machine had come apart. Order had dissolved. Something more than a political system had collapsed. The real itself seemed problematic. A life that had seemed so coherent, so inevitable, secure in its procedures, values, assumptions, disappeared overnight. David Beeves believed someone was in charge, not a businessman, to be sure, but someone, until suddenly he could no longer believe this to be true. God, it seemed, had jumped to his death.

Beyond the Depression, however, there was another source for this sense of abandonment, this sudden realization that anything could happen at any time, that there was no redeeming coherence to experience. The novel version of *The Man Who Had All the Luck* overlapped with the writing of *The Golden Years,* Miller's play about Montezuma and Cortez, and both were in part a response to events far removed from America. He was thinking then, as later, of the fact of facism. The terror that was to strike Sylvia Gellberg, in Miller's later play *Broken Glass* (1994), was prompted by Kristallnacht, in 1938, when Hitler unleashed his Brown Shirts, thereby announcing that he no longer recognized a system of law, of moral necessities and human values. Here, quite suddenly, all the comforting structures were swept away. Rationality, the whole complex of interlocking social, legal and moral obligations, were effectively declared null and void. The Jew was declared a victim whose fate was never again to be in his own hands.

As the Holocaust gathered pace, he was the ultimate embodiment of human insignificance, ordered to board the train to his own annihilation and invited to pay for the privilege as if irony would be the last emotion to be felt. Hope was sustained until the clang of the metal door and the hiss of the scattered powder sucked the souls of those seemingly born with no other fate than to die locked inside their own terror. Where were the assurances of a civilization? Where was the law? Where was God?

Seen in this context, *The Man Who Had All the Luck* seems to reflect that deep sense of abandonment felt by so many as hope was not only transmuted into its opposite but itself became a component element of absurdity. David Beeves's sense of an arbitrary good fortune is merely the other side of the same coin. His question—"Why?"—becomes the question of all. If life ends in death, where can meaning be born?

It was against this that Miller pitched his own native existentialism, his belief that man is the source of his own identity, obliged to accept responsibility for himself and the society which he joins in shaping. History, to Miller, is not some implacable force crushing the human spirit. It is made by men and can be challenged and changed by those who acknowledge this truth. And if suicide might be a logical response to a sense of abandonment, renewed commitment is no less logical. The story of David Beeves was apparently about the personal dilemma of an individual in an obscure location. For Miller, though, here and throughout his work, the private and the public were intimately connected so that the questions posed by his protagonist reach out into the world.

As he remarked, "*The Man Who Had All the Luck* tells me that in the midst of the collectivist Thirties I believed it decisive what an individual thinks and does about his life, regardless of overwhelming forces. . . . David Beeves arrives as close as he can at a workable, conditional faith in the neutrality of the world's intention toward him."[6]

The Man Who Had All the Luck is, Miller has said, "trying to weigh how much of our lives is a result of our character and how much is a result of our destiny." For him, there was "no possibility . . . to come down on one side or the other."[7] In that sense he backed off from the severity of Sartrean existentialism, which made the individual bear the full burden of responsibility for action and inaction alike. For Miller, the arbitrary nature of experience could not be denied. What was necessary was to shape it into meaning, which is, after all, precisely what he saw the writer as doing in giving form to experience.

Reviews of the play were negative or, in Miller's words, baffled, and he himself came to feel that both he and the director had failed to understand its antirealist thrust. It needed a style of presentation they never found. A note at the bottom of the *Variety Review* for November 29, 1944, announced, "Withdrawn Saturday after four performances." Since one of these was a matinee, the play ran for just three days. It was a disaster. As Miller later remarked, "Standing at the back of the house . . . I could blame nobody." It was "like music played on the wrong instrument in a false scale. . . . After the final performance and the goodbyes to the actors, it almost seemed a relief to get on the subway to Brooklyn Heights and read about the tremendous pounding of Nazi-held Europe by Allied air power. Something somewhere was real."[8]

But he never forgot *The Man Who Had All the Luck*. Inspired in part by the Depression and wartime concerns, it proved a fable capable of speaking to people in other times and other places. In 1988 a staged reading convinced him that there was still life in the play. In 1989 it was republished by a British publisher (along with *The Golden Years*) and staged by the Bristol Old Vic and the Young Vic in a production that, Miller insisted, captured "the wonder and naivete and purity of feeling of a kind of fairytale about the mystery of fate and destiny," a play that he now saw had "the bright colors of youth . . . all over it, and the fixation of youth on the future and what heaven has in mind for one's life."[9] It was favorably reviewed.

There was a further staged reading in Los Angeles, in 2000, and then a production the following year at the Williamstown Festival in Massachusetts, with Chris O'Donnell as David Beeves. It was this production that reached Broadway in 2002, fifty-eight years after the play's precipitate failure. This time *The New York Times,* which had dismissed it in 1944, welcomed it as "compelling" and asked how it could ever have been so easily dismissed over half a century earlier. *The Man Who Had All the Luck* had finally arrived.

NOTES

1. Arthur Miller, *Timebends* (London, 1987), pp. 90–91.
2. Ibid., p. 105.
3. Ibid.
4. Program note of Bristol Old Vic and Young Vic production.
5. Arthur Miller, "Afterword," *The Golden Years and The Man Who Had All the Luck* (London, 1989), p. 231.
6. Arthur Miller, "Introduction," *The Golden Years and The Man Who Had All the Luck,* pp. 8, 10.
7. Mel Gussow, "Life, He Thought, Meant Waiting for One Bad Thing," *The New York Times,* April 28, 2002, Arts, p. 9.
8. Miller, *Timebends,* pp. 104–5.
9. Program note of Bristol Old Vic and Young Vic production.

The Man Who Had
All the Luck

Cast

DAVID BEEVES
SHORY
J.B. FELLER
ANDREW FALK
PATTERSON (PAT) BEEVES
AMOS BEEVES
HESTER FALK
DAN DIBBLE
GUSTAV EBERSON
AUGIE BELFAST
AUNT BELLE

ACT ONE

Scene i

*A barn in a small, midwestern town. It is set on a rake angle.
The back wall of the barn sweeps toward upstage and right,
and the big entrance doors are in this wall. Along the left
wall a work bench on which auto tools lie along with some
old parts and rags and general mechanic's junk. A rack over
the bench holds wrenches, screwdrivers, other tools. In the
left wall is a normal-sized door leading into Shory's Feed and
Grain Store to which this barn is attached. A step-high ramp
leads down from the threshold of this door into the barn.
Further to the left, extending into the offstage area along the
wall, are piles of cement bags. In front of them several new
barrels that contain fertilizer.*

*Downstage, near the center, is a small wood stove, now
glowing red. Over the bench is a hanging bulb. There is a big
garage jack on the floor, several old nail barrels for chairs—
two of them by the stove. A large drum of alcohol lies on
blocks, downstage right. Near it are scattered a few gallon
tins. This is an old barn being used partly as a storage place,
and mainly as an auto repair shop. The timber supports have
a warm, oak color, unstained. The colors of wood dominate
the scene, and the grey of the cement bags.*

*Before the rise, two car horns, one of them the old-fashioned
ga-goo-ga type of the old Ford, are heard honking impatiently. An instant of this and the curtain rises.*

DAVID BEEVES *is filling a can from an alcohol drum. He is*

twenty-two. He has the earnest manner of the young, small-town businessman until he forgets it, which is most of the time. Then he becomes what he is—wondrous, funny, naïve, and always searching. He wears a windbreaker.

Enter J.B. FELLER *from the right. He is a fat man near fifty, dressed for winter. A certain delicacy of feeling clings to his big face. He has a light way of walking despite his weight.*

J.B.: Sure doing nice business on that alcohol, huh David? [*Thumbing right*] They're freezing out there, better step on it.

DAVID: Near every car in town's been here today for some. April! What a laugh!

J.B. [*nods downstage*]: My store got so cold I had to close off the infant's wear counter. I think I'll get a revolving door for next winter. [*Sits*] What you got your hair all slicked for?

DAVID [*on one knee, examines the spigot which pours slowly*]: Going over to Hester's in a while.

J.B.: Dave! [*Excitedly*] Going alone?

DAVID: Hester'll be here right away. I'm going to walk back to the house with her, and . . . well, I guess we'll lay down the law to him. If he's going to be my father-in-law I better start talking to him some time.

J.B. [*anxiously*]: The only thing is you want to watch your step with him.

DAVID [*turns off spigot, lifts up can as he gets to his feet*]: I can't believe that he'd actually start a battle with me. You think he would?

J.B.: Old man Falk is a very peculiar man, Dave.

Horns sound from the right.

DAVID [*going right with the can*]: Coming, coming!

He goes out as from the back door, SHORY *descends the ramp in a fury. He is in a wheelchair. He is thirty-eight but his age is hard to tell because of the absence of any hair on his body. He is totally bald, his beard does not grow, his eyebrows are gone. His face is capable of great laughter and terrible sneers. A dark green blanket covers his legs. He stops at the big doors with his fist in the air. As he speaks the horns stop.*

SHORY: Goddamn you, shut those goddam horns! Can't you wait a goddam minute?

J.B.: Lay off, will you? They're his customers.

SHORY [turns]: What're you doing, living here?

J.B.: Why, got any objections? [Goes to stove, clapping his arms.] Jesus, how can he work in this place? You could hang meat in here. [Warms his hands on the stove.]

SHORY: You cold with all that fat on you?

J.B.: I don't know why everybody thinks a fat man is always warm. There's nerves in the fat too, y'know.

SHORY: Come into the store. It's warmer. Shoot some pinochle. [Starts toward the ramp to his store.]

J.B.: Dave's going over to see Falk.

SHORY stops.

SHORY: Dave's not going to Falk.

J.B.: He just told me.

SHORY [turns again]: Listen. Since the day he walked into the store and asked me for a job he's been planning on going to see Falk about Hester. That's seven years of procrastination, and it ain't going to end tonight. What is it with you lately? You hang around him like an old cow or something. What'd your wife throw you out of the house again?

J.B.: No, I don't drink anymore, not any important drinking—really. [He sits on a barrel.] I keep thinking about those two kids. It's so rare. Two people staying in love since they were children . . . that oughtn't to be trifled with.

SHORY: Your wife did throw you out, didn't she?

J.B.: No, but . . . we just got the last word: no kids.

SHORY [compassionately]: That so, Doctor?

J.B.: Yeh, no kids. Too old. Big, nice store with thirty-one different departments. Beautiful house. No kids. Isn't that something? You die, and they wipe your name off the mail box and . . . and that's the ball game.

Slight pause.

[Changing the subject; with some relish.] I think I might be able to put Dave next to something very nice, Shor.

SHORY: You're in your dotage, you know that? You're getting a Santa Claus complex.

J.B.: No, he just reminds me of somebody. Myself, in fact. At his age I was in a roaring confusion. And him? He's got his whole life laid out like a piece of linoleum. I don't know why but sometimes I'm around him and it's like watching one of them nice movies, where you know everything is going to turn out good . . . [*Suddenly strikes him.*] I guess it's because he's so young . . . and I'm gettin' so goddam old.

SHORY: What's this you're puttin' him next to?

J.B.: My brother-in-law up in Burley; you know, Dan Dibble that's got the mink ranch.

SHORY: Oh don't bring him around, now . . .

J.B.: Listen, his car's on the bum and he's lookin' for a mechanic. He's a sucker for a mechanic!

SHORY: That hayseed couldn't let go of a nickel if it was stuck up his . . .

Roar of engines starting close by outside. Enter DAVID *from the upstage door, putting a small wrench in his pocket. As he comes in two cars are heard pulling away. He goes to a can of gasoline and rinses his hands.*

DAVID: Geez, you'd think people could tighten a fan belt. What time you got, John?

SHORY: Why, where *you* going? You can't go into Falk's house . . .

From the store enter AUNT BELLE. *She is carrying a wrapped shirt and a bag. She is a woman who was never young; skinny, bird-like, constantly sniveling. A kerchief grows out of her hand.*

BELLE: I thought you were in the store. Hester said to hurry.

DAVID [*going to her*]: Oh, thanks, Belle. [*Unwrapping a shirt.*] It's the new one, isn't it?

BELLE [*horrified*]: Did you want the new one?

DAVID [*looking at the shirt*]: Oh, Belle. When are you going to remember something! Hester told you to bring my new shirt!

BELLE [*lifting them out of bag*]: Well I—I brought your galoshes.

DAVID: I don't wear galoshes anymore, I wanted my new shirt! Belle, sometimes you . . .

BELLE *bursts into tears.*

All right, all right, forget it.

BELLE: I only do my best, I'm not your mother . . .

DAVID [*leading her right*]: I'm sorry, Aunt Belle, go—and thanks.

BELLE [*still sniffling*]: Your father's got your brother Amos out running on the road . . .

DAVID: Yeah, well . . . thanks . . .

BELLE [*a kerchief at her nose*]: He makes Amos put on his galoshes, why doesn't he give a thought to you?

DAVID [*pats her hand*]: I'll be home later.

SHORY: You know why you never remember anything, Belle? You blow your nose too much. The nose is connected with the brain and you're blowin' your brains out.

DAVID: Ah, cut it out, will ya?

With another sob, BELLE *rushes out.*

She still treats me like after Mom died. Just like I was seven years old. [DAVID *picks up the clean shirt.*]

SHORY [*alarmed*]: Listen, that man'll kill you. [*Grabs the shirt and sits on it.*]

DAVID [*with an embarrassed but determined laugh, trying to grab the shirt back*]: Give me that. I decided to go see him, and I'm going to see him!

Enter PAT *and* AMOS *from right.* PAT *is a small, nervous man about forty-five,* AMOS *is twenty-four, given to a drawl and a tendency to lumber when he walks.*

PAT [*on entering*]: What's the matter with you?

DAVID *looks up.* ALL *turn to him as both come center.* AMOS *is squeezing a rubber ball.*

[*Pointing between* DAVID *and stove*]: Don't you know better than to stand so close to that stove? Heat is ruination to the arteries.

AMOS [*eagerly*]: You goin', Dave?

SHORY [*to* PAT]: Everything was getting clear. Will you go home?

PAT: I'm his father, if you please.

SHORY: Then tell him what to do, father.

PAT: I'll tell him. [*Turns to* DAVID *as though to command.*] What exactly did you decide?

DAVID: We're going to tell Mr. Andrew Falk we're getting married.

PAT: Uh, huh. Good work.

SHORY: Good work! [*Pointing at* PAT, *he turns to* J.B.] Will you listen to this . . . !

J.B. [*he shares* SHORY's *attitude toward* PAT, *but with more compassion*]: But somebody ought to go along with him.

PAT [*adamantly to* DAVID]: Definitely, somebody ought to go along . . .

AMOS [*to* DAVID]: Let me go. If he starts anything, I'll . . .

DAVID [*to* ALL]: Now look, for Christ's sake, will you . . .

PAT [*to* DAVID]: I forbid you to curse. Close your collar, Amos. [*Of* AMOS *to* J.B.] Just ran two miles. [*He buttons another button on* AMOS, *indicating Amos's ball.*] How do you like the new method?

AMOS [*holds up ball*]: Squeezin' a rubber ball.

J.B.: What's that, for his fingers, heh?

DAVID *examines his arm.*

PAT: Fingers! That's the old forearm. A pitcher can have everything, but without a forearm?—Zero!

SHORY [*to* PAT, *of* DAVE]: Are you going to settle this or is he going to get himself murdered in that house?

PAT: Who? What house? [*Recalling.*] Oh yes, Dave . . .

SHORY [*to* J.B.]: Oh yes, Dave! [*To* PAT.] You're his father, for G . . . !

DAVID: All right. I got enough advice. Hester's coming here right away and we're going over to the house and we'll talk it out, and if . . .

SHORY: His brains are busted, how are you going to talk to him? He doesn't like you, he doesn't want you, he said he'd shoot you if you came onto his place. Now will you start from there and figure it out or you going to put it together in the hospital? [*Pause.*]

DAVID: What am I supposed to do then? Let him send her to that normal school? I might never see her again. I know how these things work.

SHORY: You don't know how these things work. Two years I waited in there for a boy to ask for the job I put up in the window. I could've made a big stink about it. I was a veteran, people ought to explain to the kids why I looked like this.

But I learned something across the sea. Never go lookin' for trouble. I waited. And you came. Wait, Davey.

PAT: I'm inclined to agree with him, David.

DAVID: I've been waiting to marry Hester since we were babies. [*Sits on a barrel.*] God! How do you know when to wait and when to take things in your hand and make them happen?

SHORY: You can't make anything happen any more than a jellyfish makes the tides, David.

DAVID: What do you say, John?

J.B.: I'd hate to see you battle old man Falk, but personally, Dave, I don't believe in waiting too long. A man's got to have faith, I think, and push right out into the current, and . . .

PAT [*leans forward, pointing*]: Faith, David, is a great thing. Take me for instance. When I came back from the sea . . .

DAVID: What time you got, John . . . excuse me, Dad.

J.B.: Twenty to eight.

DAVID [*to* SHORY]: You giving me that shirt or must I push you off that chair?

PAT [*continuing*]: I am speaking, David. When I came back from the sea . . .

SHORY [*pointing at* AMOS]: Before you come back from the sea, you're going to kill him, running his ass off into the snow.

PAT: Kill him! Why it's common knowledge that pacing is indispensable for the arches. After all, a pitcher can have everything, but if his arches are not perfect . . . ?

SHORY: Zero!

PAT: Before I forget, do you know if that alcohol can be used for rubbing? [*Indicates the drum.*]

DAVID: There's only a couple of drops left.

AMOS: You sold it all today? [*Joyously to* PAT.] I told you he'd sell it all!

DAVID: Don't go making a genius out of your brother. Salesman hooked him. He bought alcohol in April when the sun was shining hot as hell.

AMOS: Yeah, but look how it froze up today!

SHORY: *He* didn't know it was going to freeze.

J.B.: Maybe he did know. [*To* DAVE.] Did you, Dave?

DAVID [*stares into his memory*]: Well, I . . . I kinda thought . . .

PAT [*breaking in*]: Speaking of geniuses, most people didn't know that there are two kinds; physical and mental. Take pitchers like Christy Matthewson now. Or Walter Johnson. There you have it in a nutshell. Am I right, J.B.?

SHORY: What've you got in a nutshell?

PAT [*the beginnings of confusion, his desire to protect* AMOS *and himself against everyone, tremble in him*]: Just what I said. People simply refuse to concentrate. They don't know what they're supposed to be doing in their lives.

SHORY [*pointing to* DAVID]: Example number one.

PAT [*rises to a self-induced froth of a climax*]: I always left David to concentrate for himself. But take Amos then. When I got back from the sea I came home and what do I find? An infant in his mother's arms. I felt his body and I saw it was strong. And I said to myself, this boy is not going to waste out his life being seventeen different kind of things and ending up nothing. He's going to play baseball. And by ginger he's been throwin' against the target down the cellar seven days a week for twelve solid years! That's concentration. That's faith! That's taking your life in your own hands and molding it to fit the thing you want. That's bound to have an effect . . . and don't you think they don't know it!

SHORY: Who knows it?

PAT [*with a cry*]: I don't like everybody's attitude! [*Silence an instant.* ALL *staring at him.*] It's still winter! Can he play in the winter?

SHORY: Who are you talking about?

DAVID [*going away—toward the right—bored and disgusted*]: Dad, he didn't say . . .

PAT: He doesn't have to say it. You people seem to think he's going to go through life pitching Sundays in the sand lots. [*To* ALL.] Pitching's his business; it's a regular business like . . . like running a store, or being a mechanic or anything else. And it happens that in the winter there is nothing to do in his business but sit home and wait!

J.B.: Well, yeh, Pat, that's just what he ought to be doing.

PAT: Then why does everybody look at him as though . . . ?

He raises his hand to his head, utterly confused and ashamed for his outburst. A long pause like this.

DAVID [*unable to bear it, he goes to* PAT]: Sit down, Dad. Sit down. [*He gets a barrel under* PAT, *who sits, staring, exhausted.*]

PAT: I can't understand it. Every paper in the county calls him a phenomenon.

As he speaks, DAVID, *feeling* PAT's *pain, goes right a few yards and stands looking away.*

Undefeated. He's ready for the big leagues. Been ready for three years. Who can explain a thing like that? Why don't they send a scout?

DAVID: I been thinking about that, Dad. Maybe you ought to call the Detroit Tigers again.

AMOS [*peevishly. This has been in him a long time*]: He never called them in the first place.

PAT: Now, Amos . . .

DAVID [*reprimanding*]: Dad . . .

AMOS: He didn't. He didn't call them. [*To* PAT.] I want him to know!

DAVID [*to* PAT]: But last summer you said . . .

PAT: I've picked up the phone a lot of times . . . but I . . . I wanted it to happen . . . naturally. It ought to happen naturally, Dave.

SHORY: You mean you don't want to hear them say no.

PAT: Well . . . yes, I admit that. [*To* DAVID.] If I call now and demand an answer, maybe they'll have to say no. I don't want to put that word in their head in relation to Amos. It's a great psychological thing there. Once they refuse it's twice as hard to get them to accept.

DAVID: But, Dad, maybe . . . maybe they forgot to send a scout. Maybe they even thought they'd sent one and didn't, and when you call they'll thank you for reminding them. [*To* ALL.] I mean . . . can you *just wait for something to happen?*

SHORY [*claps*]: Pinochle? Let's go. Come on, John! Pat!

They start for the store door.

J.B. [*glancing at his watch*]: My wife'll murder me.

SHORY: Why? Pinochle leaves no odor on the breath.

PAT [*turning at ramp*]: I want you to watch us, Amos. Pinochle is very good for the figuring sense. Help you on base play. Open your coat.

PAT *follows* SHORY *and* J.B. *into the store.* AMOS *dutifully starts to follow, hesitates at the door, then closes it behind them and comes to* DAVID.

AMOS: Dave, I want to ask you something. [*He glances toward the door, then quietly.*] Take me over, will ya? [DAVE *just looks at him.*] Do something for me. I'm standing still. I'm not going anywhere. I swear I'm gettin' ashamed.

DAVID: Ah, don't, don't, Ame.

AMOS: No, I am. Since I started to play everybody's been saying, [*Mimics.*] "Amos is goin' someplace, Amos is goin' someplace." I been out of high school five years and I'm still taking spending money. I want to find a girl. I want to get married. I want to start doing things. You're movin' like a daisy cutter, Dave, you know how to *do*. Take me over.

DAVID: But I don't know half what Pop knows about baseball . . . about training or . . .

AMOS: I don't care, you didn't know anything about cars either, and look what you made here.

DAVID: What'd I make? I got nothin'. I still don't know anything about cars.

AMOS: But you do. Everybody knows you know . . .

DAVID: Everybody's crazy. Don't envy me, Ame. If every car I ever fixed came rolling in here tomorrow morning and the guys said I did it wrong I wouldn't be surprised. I started on Shory's Ford and I got another one and another, and before I knew what was happening they called me a mechanic. But I ain't a trained man. You are. You *got* something . . . [*Takes his arm, with deepest feeling.*] and you're going to be great. Because you deserve it. You know something perfect. Don't look to me, I could be out on that street tomorrow morning, and then I wouldn't look so smart. . . . Don't laugh at Pop. You're his whole life, Ame. You hear me? You stay with him.

AMOS: Gee, Dave . . . you always make me feel so good. [*Sud-*

denly like PAT, *ecstatic.*] When I'm in the Leagues I'm gonna buy you . . . a . . . a whole goddam garage!

Enter HESTER *from the right. She is a full-grown girl, a heartily developed girl. She can run fast, swim hard, and lift heavy things—not stylishly—with the most economical and direct way to run, swim and lift. She has a loud, throaty laugh. Her femininity dwells in one fact—she loves* DAVID *with all her might, always has, and she doesn't feel she's doing anything when he's not around. The pallor of tragedy is nowhere near her. She enters breathless, not from running but from expectation.*

HESTER: David, he's home. [*Goes to* DAVID *and cups his face in her hands.*] He just came back! You ready? [*Looks around* DAVID's *shoulder at* AMOS.] Hullo, Ame, how's the arm?

AMOS: Good as ever.

HESTER: You do that long division I gave you?

AMOS: Well, I been working at it.

HESTER: There's nothing better'n arithmetic to sharpen you up. You'll see, when you get on the diamond again, you'll be quicker on base play. We better go, David.

AMOS [*awkwardly*]: Well . . . good luck to ya. [*He goes to the store door.*]

DAVID: Thanks, Ame.

AMOS *waves, goes through the door and closes it behind him.*

HESTER: What're you looking so pruney about? Don't you want to go?

DAVID: I'm scared, Hess. I don't mind tellin' you. I'm scared.

HESTER: Of a beatin'?

DAVID: You know I was never scared of a beatin'.

HESTER: We always knew we'd have to tell him, didn't we?

DAVID: Yeh, but I always thought that by the time we had to, I'd be somebody. You know . . .

HESTER: But you are somebody . . .

DAVID: But just think of it from his side. He's a big farmer, a hundred and ten of the best acres in the county. Supposing he asks me—I only got three hundred and ninety-four dollars, counting today . . .

house and never uses nothin' but a broom. Now listen. He claims she ain't hitting right. I been tryin' the past two weeks to get him to bring her down here to you. Now get this. Besides the mink ranch he's got a wheat farm with five tractors.

HESTER: Five tractors!

J.B.: He's an idiot, but he's made a fortune out of mink. Now you clean up this Marmon for him and you'll open your door to the biggest tractor farms in the state. There's big money in tractor work, you know that. He's got a thousand friends and they follow him. They'll follow him here.

DAVID: Uh, huh. But I don't know anything about tractors.

HESTER: Oh, heck, you'll learn!

DAVID: Yeah, but I can't learn on his tractors.

HESTER: Yeah, but . . .

J.B.: Listen! This could be the biggest thing that ever happened to you. The Marmon's over at my house. He's afraid to drive her any further on the snow. I'll bring her over and you'll go to work. All right?

DAVID: Yeah, but look, John, I . . .

J.B.: You better get in early and start on her first thing in the morning. All right?

HESTER [*with a loud bubble of laughter*]: David, that's wonderful!

DAVID [*quickly*]: See, if we waited, Hess. In six months, maybe less, I'd have something to show!

HESTER: But I'm going to Normal in a week if we don't do it now!

SHORY: You're pushing him, Hester.

HESTER [*a sudden outburst at* SHORY]: Stop talking to him! A person isn't a frog, to wait and wait for something to happen!

SHORY: He'll fight your father if you drag him there tonight! And your father can kill him!

DAVID [*takes her hand. Evenly*]: Come on, Hess. We'll go. [*To* J.B.] Bring the car over, I'll be back later . . .

But J.B. *is staring off right, down the driveway.* DAVE *turns, with* HESTER *and all to follow his stare. She steps a foot away from him. Enter* ANDREW FALK, *a tall, old man, hard as iron, nearsighted, slightly stooped. Sound of idling motor outside.*

J.B. [*after a moment*]: I'll bring the car, Dave. Five minutes.

DAVID [*affecting a businesslike, careless flair*]: Right, J.B., I'll fix him up. [*as* J.B. *goes out.*] And thanks loads, John!

FALK *has been looking at* HESTER, *who dares every other moment to look up from the floor at him.* DAVID *turns to* FALK, *desperately controlling his voice.* PAT *enters from* SHORY'*s store.*

Evening, Mr. Falk. You want to go in to Shory's store? There's chairs there . . . [FALK *turns deliberately, heavily looks at him.*] You left your engine running. Stay awhile. Let me shut it off.

FALK: You willin' to push it?

DAVID: Oh, battery run down?

FALK [*caustically*]: I don't know what else would prevent her from turnin' over without a push. [*To* HESTER.] I'll see you home.

HESTER [*smiling, she goes to him, but does not touch him*]: We were just comin' to the house, Daddy.

FALK: Go on home, Hester.

DAVID: We'd like to talk to you, Mr. Falk. [*Indicating the store.*] We could all go . . .

FALK [*in reply*]: Go on home, Hester.

DAVID [*with a swipe at indignation*]: I'd like for her to be here, Mr. Falk . . .

FALK [*he does not even look at David*]: I'll be home right away. [*He takes her arm and moves her to the right. She digs her heels in.*]

HESTER [*a cry*]: Daddy, why . . . !

She breaks off, looking into his face. With a sob she breaks from him and runs off right. He turns slowly to DAVID, *takes a breath.*

DAVID [*angering*]: That ain't gonna work any more, Mr. Falk. We're old enough now.

PAT [*reasonably*]: Look, Falk, why don't we . . . ?

FALK [*to* DAVID, *without so much as a glance at* PAT]: This is the last time I'm ever goin' to talk to you, Beeves. You . . .

DAVID: Why is it you're the only man who hates me like this? Everybody else . . .

FALK: Nobody but me knows what you are.

SHORY [*from the store doorway*]: What is he? What are you blowin' off about?

FALK [*his first rise of voice. He points at* SHORY]: The good God gave you your answer long ago! Keep your black tongue in your head when I'm here.

SHORY [*nervously. To* DAVID]: His brains are swimmin', don't you see? What are you botherin' with him for . . . !

FALK [*roaring, he takes a stride toward* SHORY]: Shut up, you . . . you whoremonger! You ruined your last woman on *this* earth! The good God saw to that.

SHORY [*with a screech of fury*]: You don't scare me, Falk. You been dead twenty years, why don't you bury yourself?

FALK *strangely relaxes, walks away from* SHORY'S *direction, raising his shoulder to run his chin on his coat collar. The motor outside stalls. His head cocks toward right.*

DAVID [*pointing to the right*]: Your car stalled. I'll start her up for you.

FALK: Don't touch anything I own! [*Pause.*] What were you doin' that night I caught you with her by the river? You got backbone enough to tell me that?

DAVID [*recalls*]: Oh . . . we were kids then . . . just talkin', that's all.

FALK: You never come and ask me if she could talk to you. You come sneakin' every time, like a rat through the fences.

DAVID: Well . . . Hess was always scared to ask you, and I . . . I guess I got it from her.

FALK: You're scared of me now too, and you know why, Beeves? Nobody but me knows what you are.

DAVID: Why, what am I?

FALK: You're a lost soul, a lost man. You don't know the nights I've watched you, sittin' on the river ice, fishin' through a hole—alone, alone like an old man with a boy's face. Or makin' you a fire in Keldon's woods where nobody could see. And that Sunday night you nearly burned down the church . . .

DAVID: I was nowhere near the church that night . . . !

FALK: It couldn't have been nobody else! When the church burned there never was a sign from God that was so clear.

AMOS: He was down in the cellar with me when the church
burned.

FALK [*looks at* AMOS]: I am not blind. [*Turns back to* DAVID.]
The man Hester marries is gonna know what he's about.
He's gonna be a steady man that I can trust with what I
brought forth in this world. He's gonna know his God, he's
gonna know where he came from and where he's goin'. You
ain't that man. [*He turns to go.*]

DAVID: I'm marryin' Hester, Mr. Falk. [FALK *stops, turns.*] I'm
sorry, but we're going to marry.

FALK: Beeves, if you ever step onto my land again, I'll put a
bullet through you, may God write my words . . . I don't
fool, Beeves. Don't go near her again. [*Points to* SHORY.] No
man who could find a friend in that lump of corruption is going to live in my daughter's house. [*He starts to go again.*]

DAVID: I'm marryin' Hester, Mr. Falk! We're gonna do it!

FALK: You'll sleep with your shroud first, Beeves. I'm old
enough to know what I'll do. Stay away!

*He goes to the right edge of the stage, and hesitates, looking
off right in the direction of his stalled car.* DAVID *starts
doubtfully toward him, looking over his shoulder.*

SHORY [*rolling down the ramp*]: Let him start it himself! Don't
be a damned fool!

FALK *hurries out.*

PAT [*pointing right*]: Maybe you ought to give him a push.

SHORY: Not on your life! [*He pushes himself between* DAVE
and the door.] Get away from there, go on!

DAVID [*looking off right all the time*]: Shory . . . he's going . . .
what can I say to him . . . [*Starts to go right.*] I'll help him.

SHORY [*pushes him back*]: Get away! [*Calling off right.*] That's
it, Grandpa, push it . . . push it! Harder, you crazy bastard,
it's only half a mile! Go ahead, harder! [*Laughs wildly,
mockingly.*]

DAVID [*wrenches the chair around*]: Stop it!

SHORY: You can't talk to that man! You're through, you
damned fool.

DAVID [*suddenly*]: Come on, Ame, we'll pick up Hester on the

road before he gets home. I'm going to do it tonight, by
God . . .

AMOS [*in ecstasy at the thought of action, he wings the ball
across the stage*]. Let's go!

PAT [*grabs* DAVID]: No, Dave . . .

DAVID [*furiously*]: No, I gotta do it, Dad!

PAT: I forbid it. [*To* AMOS.] I forbid you to go. [*To* DAVID.]
She's his daughter and he's got a right, David.

DAVID: What right has he got! *She* wants me!

PAT: Then let her break from him. That's not your province.

DAVID: She's scared to death of him! The whole thing is between me and Hester. *I don't understand why I can't have
that girl!*

SHORY [*sardonically*]: Must there be a reason?

DAVID [*he stops for an instant as though a light flashed on
him*]: Yes, there has to be a reason! I did everything a man
could do. *I didn't do anything wrong and . . .*

SHORY: You didn't have to! [DAVE *stares at* SHORY.] A man is
a jellyfish. The tide goes in and the tide goes out. About what
happens to him, a man has very little to say. When are you
going to get used to it?

DAVID *stands staring.*

PAT: You better go home and sleep, Dave. Sleep is a great doctor, you know.

SHORY [*gently*]: He said it, Dave.

Enter J.B. *in a hurry.*

J.B.: Where is Dan? Where's the Marmon?

PAT: He didn't come here.

J.B.: That ox! I tell him I'll drive it over for him. No, Dan Dibble don't allow anybody behind the wheel but himself. I go
into the house to tell Ellie I'm goin' and when I come out he's
gone. [*Starts to go right.*] That seven passenger moron . . .

DAVID: He probably decided to go back home to Burley.

J.B.: No, I'm sure he's tryin' to get here. Rugged individualist!
I'll find him on some dirt road some place . . . [*He shuts up
abruptly as a door slams outside.*]

All look right.

DAVID [*alarmed*]: Hester!

He quickly goes off right. For an instant AMOS, PAT, *and* SHORY *are galvanized.* AMOS *goes off and returns immediately supporting* DAN DIBBLE *who is shaking all over and seems about to collapse in distress.*

DIBBLE [*on entering*]: God help me, God in Heaven help me . . .

Enter DAVID *and* J.B. *helping* HESTER. *She is sobbing on* DAVID's *arm and he's trying to lift her face up.*

DAVID: Stop crying, what' the matter? Hester, stop it, what happened? J.B.!

DIBBLE [*goes prayerfully to* HESTER]: I couldn't see him, Miss, how in the world could I see him? His car had no lights . . .

HESTER's *loud sob cuts him off.*

DAVID [*to* DAN]: What happened? What did you do?

DIBBLE: Oh, God in Heaven, help me . . .

J.B. [*goes to him, pulls his hands down*]: Dan . . . stop that. . . . For Pete's sake, what happened?

DIBBLE: This girl's father . . . an old man . . . I couldn't see him . . . He was pushing a car without lights. There were no lights at all, and he walked out from behind just as I came on him.

But for HESTER's *subsiding sobs, there is silence for a moment. She looks at* DAVID, *who looks once at her, then comes to life.*

DAVID [*to* DAN]: Where is he now?

DIBBLE [*points upstage*]: I took him to his house . . . she was there. It happened a few feet from his house.

DAVID [*horrified*]: Well, why didn't you get a doctor! [*He starts for the back door.*]

HESTER: No . . . he's dead, Davey.

Almost at the ramp, DAVID *stops as though shot. After an instant he turns quickly. He comes as in a dream a few yards toward her, and, as in a dream, halts, staring at her.*

He's dead.

DAVID *stares at her. Then turns his head to* PAT, AMOS, SHORY, DAN . . . *as though to seek reality. Then looking at her once more he goes to the nail barrel and sits.*

DAVID [*whisper*]: I'll be darned. [*Goes to* HESTER . . . *after a moment.*] I'm so sorry.

HESTER: It was nobody's fault. Oh that poor man!

PAT [*goes to* DAVID]: You better . . . come home, David.

DAVID [*he gets up, goes to* HESTER, *takes her hand*]: Hess? I really am sorry.

HESTER *looks at him, a smile comes to her face. She thankfully throws her arms around him and sobs.*

Don't Hess . . . don't cry anymore. Please Hess . . . John, take her to your house for tonight, heh?

J.B.: I was going to do that. [*Takes* HESTER's *arm.*] Come on, baby. I'll tend to everything.

DAVID: Goodnight, Hess. You sleep, heh?

HESTER: You mustn't feel any fault, Davey.

DAVID: I could have gotten him started, that's all. He said . . . [*A filament of sardonic laughter.*] . . . don't touch anything I own.

HESTER: It wasn't your fault! You understand? In any way.

DAVID [*nods inconclusively*]: Go to bed, go ahead.

J.B. [*leading* HESTER *off*]: We'll get you home, and you'll sleep.

DIBBLE [DAN *follows them until he gets to the right edge. Turning to* DAVID]: If there's any blood on the car will you clean it off? Please, will you?

DAN *goes,* DAVID *looks after them.*

SHORY: Get me home, will you, Dave?

DAVID: Huh? No, I'll stay awhile. I want to look at the car. You take him, will you, Dad?

PAT [*taking hold of the back of* SHORY's *chair*]: Sure. Come on, Amos.

SHORY: Well, wake up, jellyfish. A hundred and ten of the best acres in the valley. Not bad, eh?

DAVID [*stunned*]: Just like that.

SHORY: Never happens any other way, brother. [*Almost intones it.*] Jellyfish don't swim. . . . It's the tide moves him . . . out and in . . . out and in . . . and in. Keep it in mind. [*To* PAT.] Let's go, father.

They push him out as DAVID *stands there lost in a dream. Curtain.*

Scene ii

The barn near dawn.

DAVID *is lying under the front end of the Marmon. Beside it the hood stands on end on the floor.* DAVID *is lying under the engine with one light near his head, hurriedly tightening a nut on the pan. There is one other light on, over the bench, but this is shaded. After a moment,* DAVID *hurriedly slides out from under and eagerly looking at the engine, wipes his hands. He is about to get into the car to start it when a soft knock from offstage right is heard. Startled, he peers through the darkness.*

DAVID: Who's that? [*Surprised.*] Hester . . .

HESTER [*she comes out of the darkness at right*]: Aren't you finished yet?

DAVID [*glancing defensively at the car*]: What are you doing up? What time is it?

HESTER: It's almost five. I called your house, I just couldn't sleep. Belle said you were still here. Can I watch you?

DAVID: . . . It's pretty cold in here, you'll catch cold.

HESTER [*she goes to him, takes his face in her hands, and kisses him*]: You didn't kiss me yet.

DAVID [*with growing ill-ease*]: Please, Hess, I gotta figure something out here. I wish . . . I wish you'd leave me alone for a while. Please.

HESTER [*with quiet astonishment—and compassion*]: Haven't you figured it out yet?

DAVID: Oh, I got it just about, but not . . . [*Stops.*] Hess, please leave me alone.

DAVID *walks from her and pretends to study the engine.*

HESTER: Davey.

DAVID: Ya?

HESTER: You're *going* to be able to fix it, aren't you?

DAVID: Don't you think I can?

HESTER: I know you can.

DAVID: Then why do you ask me?

HESTER: Because . . . in the Burley garage they didn't know how to fix it.

DAVID [*he straightens. Slight pause*]: How do you know?

HESTER: J.B. told me. He's going to tell you in the morning after you're finished. He didn't want to scare you about it.

DAVID [*with growing fear*]: That can't be. They got regular trained mechanics in the Burley garage.

HESTER: But it's true. Mr. Dibble said they wanted to take the whole thing apart and charge him a hundred and fifty dollars, and he wouldn't let them because . . .

DAVID [*comes to her anxiously*]: Why'd they want to take the whole thing apart?

HESTER [*seeing his bewilderment clearer*]: Well, I don't know, Davey . . .

DAVID: Well, what'd they tell him was wrong? Don't you remember . . . ?

HESTER [*her sob threatening*]: Well, Davey, don't shout at me that way, I don't know anything about cars . . . [*She begins to cry.*]

DAVID [*with the pain of guilt*]: Oh, Hester, don't cry, please. I'll fix it, I'll find out what the matter is, please, stop it, will you? *The pain it causes him makes him turn and almost march to the car. On the point of weeping himself.*

I never *heard* an engine make that sound. I took the pan off, I took the head off, I looked at the valves; I just don't know what it is, Hess! It's turning off-center somewhere and I can't find it, I can't!

HESTER [*her sobbing vanishes as she senses his loss*]: That's all right, Davey, it'll be all right. Maybe you better go to bed. You look so tired . . . It really doesn't matter so much.

DAVID [*she growing taller upon his guilt.*]: Gosh, Hess . . . there never was a girl like you. [*He goes to her and kisses her.*] I swear there never was.

HESTER: Don't ever try for anything I want, if it worries you too much to get it, Davey.

DAVID [*he kisses her cheek. With swift resolution*]: You go home and go to bed. I'll find out what's the matter. I'll do it! You go.

HESTER: All right, Davey, 'cause J.B. was telling Mr. Dibble such great things about you. . . . He's got a marvelous thing to tell you in the morning.

DAVID: What?

HESTER: I can't tell you till you finish . . .

DAVID: Please, Hess, what'd he say?

HESTER: No, fix it first. [*Pause.*] J.B. wants to tell you himself. He made me promise. Goodnight.

DAVID: Goodnight, Hess.

HESTER [*going and waving*]: And don't worry . . . about anything, okay?

DAVID: . . . I won't.

He watches her go, then turns to the car, goes and stands over it, tapping his nose with his finger thoughtfully. Then lightly punching his fist into his palm in the heartbeat rhythm, faster, then faster . . . then . . . bursting out in loud whisper.

God damn!

The sound of a man walking into the shop rather slowly from offstage right is heard. DAVID *turns toward the sound and stands still watching.* GUSTAV EBERSON *enters. He is a strong man, his suit is pressed but too small for him. He wears a white shirt. A plain brown overcoat. He is smiling warmly, but with the self-effacing manner of an intruder.* DAVID *says nothing as he approaches.*

GUS [*a slight German accent*]: Excuse me, are you Mr. Beeves?

DAVID: Yeh. [*Slight pause.*]

GUS: My name is Eberson . . . Gus Eberson . . . [*With an apologetic nod and smile.*] Are you very busy? I could of course come back. Four o'clock in the morning is not the best time to visit.

DAVID: I'm busy . . . but what can I do for you?

GUS: I moved into town last night. And I couldn't wait to see my first morning. I noticed your light. I thought we ought to know each other.

DAVID [*taken*]: I'm glad to know you. I was almost hoping you were a hold-up man and you'd knock me unconscious.

GUS: I didn't mean to walk in so invisibly; I am opening a repair garage on the other end of the avenue.

DAVID: Repair garage? You mean to repair cars?

GUS [*earnestly, worriedly*]: I want to assure you, Mr. Beeves, that if I didn't think there is plenty of business here for both of us I would never set up a place in this town.

DAVID [*a faint tightness cramps his voice*]: Oh, there's plenty of business for two here. Plenty! Where is your shop?

GUS: Over there on Poplar Street, right next to the grocery store.

DAVID: Oh, that place. Gosh, nobody's been in that building for years. We used to say it was haunted.

GUS: Maybe it is! [*Laughs lightly at himself.*] I have very little machinery. As a matter of fact . . . [*Quite happily.*] . . . I have very little money too. So possibly I will not be troubling you very long.

DAVID [*with emphatic assurance*]: Oh, you'll make out all right. [*Vaguely indicates the shop.*] There's nothing to it. You come from around here?

GUS: No, I was with the Ford's Company, the River Rouge plant for several years. This last year and four months I was by the Hudson Motor people.

DAVID [*breathlessly*]: Well . . . I guess you oughta know your stuff.

GUS [*sensing . . . extra hearty, therefore*]: What is there to know? You are probably much better than I am!

DAVID: No, that's all right, I just meant . . .

GUS: I am not in the world to become rich. I was doing very well in Detroit.

DAVID: Then why'd you come here?

GUS: It is my nature. I cannot get used, I shall run, run, run, I shall work, work, work, all the time rushing. To tell you the truth, I was five years with Ford's and not one good friend did I have. Here, I hope, it will be more conducive to such activities as I always enjoy. A small town and so forth. I am Austrian, you understand. . . . Meanwhile I hope you will not object too strongly of my arrival?

DAVID [*entranced*]: Hell no. Lots of luck to you! I got no right to object. [*Extends his hand jerkily.*]

GUS [*shakes hands*]: Rights is not the question. I want to be welcome. Otherwise I will . . .

DAVID [*softly;* GUS *holds onto his hand*]: No. . . . You're welcome here. . . . You are.

GUS: Thank you. . . . Thank you.

Laughs softly, thankfully. Their hands part. GUS *turns a slow full circle looking at the shop.* DAVID *watches him like a vision. At last the Austrian faces him again. Quietly.*

How old are you?

DAVID: Goin' on twenty-two.

GUS [*indicating the car, the shop . . . everything*]: How . . . how did you know what to do? You studied somewhere mechanics?

DAVID [*with pride and yet uneasiness. The Austrian has grown very tall in his eyes*]: Oh no—I just picked it up kinda. [*Wanders near the Marmon as though to hide it.*] But I guess I got plenty to learn.

GUS: No, no! The best mechanics is made in this fashion. You must not feel at all . . . how shall I say . . . at a loss.

Pause. They hold each other's gaze in a moment of understanding. Slowly the Austrian's eyes turn toward the Marmon. DAVID, *as though relinquishing it, moves aside now, not screening it any longer.*

What's his trouble?

DAVID [*still entranced, and yet he must laugh as he confesses*]: You got me there. I've been at it all night . . .

GUS [*sauntering easily to the car*]: Oh? What he complains of?

DAVID [*for a moment he holds back; then the last shred of resentment fades and he bursts out*]: She runs with a peculiar kind of a shudder . . . like a rubbing somewhere inside.

GUS: She misfires?

DAVID: That's what's so funny. She fires on eight and the carburetor's set right on the button.

Pause. GUS *looks down at the engine.* DAVID *is bent over watching his face.*

GUS: If you . . . feel like it, you can start the engine.

DAVID [*looks at him in silence*]: You . . . you know what it is?

GUS [*reaches to him quickly*]: Look, boy, tell me and I will leave the town, I'll never come back.

DAVID: No, no . . . I want it to be . . . just the way it ought to be, the way it . . . happened.

DAVID *goes to the car door, gets in—starts the motor. The Austrian stands listening for five seconds, then snaps his hand for the motor to be switched off. It is quiet again.* DAVID *comes slowly out of the car and stands beside the Austrian, watching him.*

GUS: It is very rare. In a car so new. It comes sometimes with the Marmon, however.

DAVID [*softly*]: What is it?

GUS [*turns straight to him*]: The crankshaft is sprung.

DAVID [*for a long moment he stares into the Austrian's face*]: How could you tell by listening?

GUS: Same way you do for pistons. You know. You going to work now?

DAVID [*looks at the car*]: Ya.

He hurries around the front of the car, picks up a wrench, comes around and sets the wrench on a heat nut and starts forcing it.

GUS [*hesitates for a moment, then lays his hand on* DAVID]: Don't take the head off. [DAVID *stops.*] I mean . . . you don't need to, necessarily. [DAVID *stops moving. The wrench clatters out of his hand. He stands nearly trembling before the Austrian, who suddenly turns.*] I'll go.

DAVID [*stops him*]: No, I always knew a time would come when . . . this would happen. I mean somebody like you would come, and then I'd just . . . pack up. I knew it all the time . . .

GUS: That's nonsense. You fixed plenty cars no doubt; you're a mechanic . . .

DAVID: No, I'm not really. I don't know anything about metals and ratios and . . . I was almost going to tow it to the shop in Newton. Would you tell me what to do?

GUS: Gladly. And maybe sometimes I need a hand you'll drop by. All right?

DAVID: Oh I'd be glad to.

GUS [*grips his shoulder and points under the car*]: First you take the pan down.

DAVID [*slight pause.*]: Ya?

GUS: Then you drop the bearings. Label them so you know where to put them back.

DAVID: Ya?

GUS: Then you drop the main bearings for the crankshaft.

DAVID: Ya?

GUS: Then you drop the shaft itself. Take it up to Newton, is a good shop there. Tell them to exchange for a new shaft.

DAVID: Can't I straighten this one?

GUS: Is not possible for you.

DAVID: Could you straighten it?

GUS: That would depend—but I sold my instruments for this. You go to work now. Go ahead.

DAVID [*starts to move*]: You in a hurry to go away?

GUS: I'll stay, I'll watch you.

DAVID [*thankfully*]: Okay. [*He gets down on his knees and is about to get under the car.*] You feel like workin'? Just for a couple of minutes?

GUS: You would like me to?

DAVID: I always wanted to see how somebody else works. Y'know?

GUS: All right, come on. We rip her open. [*He pulls off his coat.*] You got a socket, a quarter inch?

DAVID [*a new excitement in him*]: I ain't got sockets yet, but . . .

GUS: That's all right, give me an open end. [DAVID *goes for the wrench quickly.*] How much oil you got in here?

DAVID [*finding the wrench*]: Just a couple of quarts. I just ran her a minute. I'll drain her.

He gets under the car quickly, opening the drain nuts, setting a can under it, as . . .

GUS: Are you married?

DAVID: Not yet . . . [*Under the car.*] but pretty soon . . . are you?

GUS [*ready to work, he kneels on one knee beside the car*]: No, but I am always hopeful. There is a nice red-headed girl in this town? [*Preparing to slide under.*]

DAVID [*laughs*]: She got to be red-headed?

GUS: Yes, I would prefer such a color. It always seemed to me in a small American town would be many red-headed girls.

Probably this is because in general I like a small town. When this car has to be ready? [*Slides under.*]

DAVID *moves to make room; sits on his heels beside the car.*

DAVID: Eleven in the morning, if possible. You think it can?

GUS: Oh, plenty of time. You got a car to take this shaft to Newton?

DAVID: Yeh, that Ford outside. Oh—my back.

GUS: Spread out, take it easy.

DAVID [*relaxes on the floor*]: Gosh, you sure swing that wrench. Lots of time I do something and I wonder how they'd do it in the factory—you know, officially.

GUS: In the factory also they wonder sometimes how it's done officially.

DAVID [*laughs*]: Yeh, I bet. [*Pause.* GUS *works.*] Gosh, I suddenly feel awful tired. I been at it all night, y'know?

GUS: Sleep, go ahead. I'll wake you when it gets interesting.

DAVID: . . . Don't think you're doing this for nothing; I'll split the bill with you.

GUS: Nonsense. [*Laughs.*] We'll even it up sometime. One hand washes the other.

DAVID*'s head comes down on his arm, his face toward the Austrian. For several moments* GUS *works in silence.* DAVID*'s breathing comes in longer draughts.* GUS, *noticing his eyes closed . . .*

Mr. Beeves?

DAVID *sleeps.*

GUS *comes out from under the car, gets his own coat and lays it over* DAVID *and looks down at him. A smile comes to his face, he shakes his head wondrously, and looks from* DAVID *all around the shop. Then, happily, and with a certain anticipation, he whispers . . .*

America!

He bends, slides under the car as the lights go down.

The lights come up on the same scene. From the large barn doors a wide shaft of sunlight is pouring in. DAVID *is asleep where he was before, the coat still on him. But now the car is off the jack, and the hood is in place over the engine. The tools are in a neat pile nearby.*

Enter J.B., DAN DIBBLE, HESTER, PAT *and* AMOS.

J.B. [*as they enter. To* DAN]: We're a little early, so if he needs more time you'll wait, Dan. . . . [*Looks at* DAVID. *Quietly.*] What'd he do, sleep here all night?

AMOS: Must've. He never come home.

J.B. [*to* DAN]: That's the type of character you're dealing with. I hope you don't forget to thank him.

DIBBLE [*fearfully touching the fender*]: It looks just the same as when I brought it. You think it's fixed?

HESTER *goes to* DAVID.

J.B. [*looks at* DAVID]: Don't worry, it's fixed.

HESTER: Should I wake him?

J.B.: Go ahead. I want to tell him right away.

HESTER [*bends over and shakes him lightly*]: Davey? Davey?

DAVID: Huh?

HESTER: Wake up. J.B.'s here. It's morning. [*Laughs.*] Look at him!

DAVID: Oh. [*Sits up and sees* J.B. *and* DIBBLE.]: Oh ya, ya. *He gets up quickly, catching the coat as it falls from him. He looks at the coat for an instant.*

HESTER [*fixing his shirt straight*]: Is it all done?

DAVID: What? I'm asleep yet, wait a minute. [*He rubs his head and walks a few steps.*]

J.B. [*To* DIBBLE *with a strongly possessive pride*]: That's when you're young. Sleep anywhere. Nothin' bothers you.

DAVID: What time is it?

J.B.: About half past ten.

DAVID [*astonished and frightened*]: Half past ten! Gosh, I didn't mean to sleep that long . . . ! [*Looks around, suddenly anxious.*]

HESTER [*laughs*]: You look so *funny!*

J.B.: Well, how'd you do, Dave, all finished?

DAVID: Finished? Well, uh . . . [*He looks at the car.*]

J.B.: If you're not, Dan can wait.

DAVID: Ya . . . just a second, I . . . [*He looks around the shop.*]

HESTER: Looking for your tools? They're right on the floor here.

DAVID [*he keeps looking all around for an instant. Looks at the tools*]: Oh, okay. [*He looks at the car as though it were explosive. He lifts the hood and looks at the engine as . . .*]

J.B.: How was it, tough job?

DAVID: Heh? Ya, pretty tough.

J.B.: Anything wrong . . . ?

DAVID: No, I . . . [*He gets on his knees and looks under the engine.*]

DIBBLE: Can I start her up now?

DAVID [*gets to his feet, looks at everyone as though in a dream*]: Okay, try her. Wait a minute, let me.

DIBBLE [*following him to the car door*]: Now don't dirty the upholstery . . .

J.B.: Don't worry about the upholstery, Dan, come over here.

DIBBLE [*coming to the front of car where* J.B. *and* HESTER *are*]: They always get in with their dirty clothes . . .
The engine starts. It hums smoothly, quietly. J.B. *turns proudly smiling to* DAN, *who creeps closer to it and listens.* HESTER *watches* J.B., *teetering on the edge of expectation, then watches* DAN. *After a moment the engine is shut off.* DAVID *comes out of the car, comes slowly into view, his eyes wide.*

PAT [*to* DAN, *of* DAVE]: Highly skilled, highly skilled.

J.B. [*beaming, to* DIBBLE]: Well, you damn fool?

DIBBLE [*excitedly*]: Why she does, she does sound fine. [*He snoops around the car.*]

DAVID: Look, J.B., I . . .

J.B. [*raises his fist and bangs on the fender*]: Goddamn, Dave, I always said it! You know what you did?

HESTER: Davey, J.B.'s going to . . .

J.B. [*to* HESTER]: I'm paying for it, at least let me tell it. Dan, come over here first and tell Dave what they did to you in Burley. Listen to this one, Dave. Pat, I want you to hear this. PAT *and* AMOS *come into the group.*

DIBBLE [*feeling the edge of the fender*]: I think he bumped it here.

J.B.: Oh, the hell with that, come over here and tell him. [DIBBLE *comes.*] What about that guy in Burley?

DIBBLE: Well, there's a garage in Burley does tractor work. But he's not reasonable . . .

J.B.: Tell him what he does.

DIBBLE: I brought this one to him and he says I'll have to take her plumb apart, every screw and bolt of her. He had his mind set on charging me a hundred and thirty-one dollars for the job. So, I figured it was just about time I stopped subsidizin' the Burley Garage Incorporated.

PAT: That's intelligent, Mr. Dibble.

DAVID: Did he tell you what was wrong with the car? The Burley man?

DIBBLE: Well, yes, he did, he always tells you something, but I can't. . . . Now wait a minute. . . . These things have a dingus they call a . . . a crankshaft? He said it was crooked, or busted, or dented . . .

J.B. [*laughs—to* DAVID, *then back to* DAN]: On a brand new Marmon! What the hell did he want with the crankshaft?

PAT: Scandalous.

DAVID: Look, J.B., lemme tell you . . .

J.B. [*drawing* DAVID *and* DAN *together*]: Go ahead, David. And listen to this, Dan. This is the first honest word you ever heard out of a mechanic. [*To* DAVID.] Go on, tell this poor sucker what the matter was.

DAVID *stands dumbly, looking into* J.B.*'s ecstatic face. He turns to* HESTER.

HESTER [*hardly able to stand still. Pridefully*]: Tell him, Davey!

DAVID [*turns back to* J.B. *He sighs*]: Just a lot of small things, that's all.

DAVID *walks a few steps away to a fender and absently touches it. It could be taken for modesty.* AMOS *is now to the side, resting a foot on the car bumper—watching in wonder.*

J.B.: Well? What do you say, Danny? Now you're looking at a *mechanic*!

PAT [*to* DAN, *of* DAVE]: At the age of six he fixed the plug on an iron.

DIBBLE [*goes to* DAVID]: Look, David. I have a proposition for you. Whenever there's a job to do on my tractors charge me for parts and that's all. If you'd do that for me, I could guarantee you more . . .

DAVID: I'm much obliged to you, Mr. Dibble, but I'm not tooled up for tractor work . . .

J.B.: Now wait a minute . . .

DAVID [*almost shouting with tension*]: Let me say something will you? To work on heavy engines like that, and tractors in general a man has got to be a . . . well, I'm not tooled up for it, that's all, I haven't got the machinery.

J.B. [*businesslike*]: But you've got the machinery.

HESTER: Listen to this, Davey!

DAVID *looks at him.*

J.B.: You go out and buy everything you want. Fix up this building. Lay out a concrete driveway in the front. I'll pay the bills. Give me one percent on my money. [*Roundly.*] Let me be some good in my life!

DAVID [*as though a fever were rising in him, his voice begins to soar*]: I don't know if I'm ready for that, J.B. . . . I'd have to study about tractors . . . I . . .

J.B.: Then study! Now's the *time,* Dave. You're young, strong . . . !

PAT [*to* DAN]: He's very strong.

DIBBLE [*taking out a roll*]: How much do I owe you, boy?

DAVID *looks at* DAN.

DAVID: Owe me?

J.B.: Make it sixty dollars flat, Dave. Since it wasn't as hard as we thought. [DAVID *looks at* J.B. *who won't wait for him to object.*] Sixty flat, Dan.

DIBBLE [*counts laboriously, peeling off each bill into* DAVID's *unwilling hand*]: One, two, three . . . [*Continues.*]

HESTER [*joyously amused at* DAN]: What're those, all ones?!

DIBBLE: All I carry is ones. Never can tell when you'll leave a five by mistake. [*Continues counting.*] Government ought to print different sizes.

J.B.: How's it feel to have two stars, heh, Pat? [*With a sweep of his hand.*] I can see a big red sign out there way up in the air. Dave Beeves, Incorporated, Tractor Station . . .

HESTER *has noticed the coat beside the car.*

HESTER [*holding the coat up*]: Did you get a new coat?

DIBBLE *continues counting into* DAVID'S *hand.*

DAVID: Huh?

Quickly turns to HESTER *and the coat.* DAN DIBBLE *continues counting.* DAVID *stares at the coat, suddenly in the full blast of all the facts. Now all but* DIBBLE *are looking at the coat.*

AMOS [*feels the coat*]: Where'd you get this?

DIBBLE: Hold still! Fifty-three, fifty-four, fifty . . .

DAVID *looks at* AMOS, *then down at his hand into which the money is still dropping. He then looks again at* AMOS . . . AMOS *to him.*

AMOS: What's the matter?

HESTER: What's come over you?

DAVID *suddenly hands the money to* HESTER.

DIBBLE: Say!

DAVID [*his hand recedes from the bills as though they were burning. To* HESTER]: Take it, will ya? I . . .

He starts to point somewhere off right as though he were being called. Then his hand drops . . . and with gathering speed he strides out.

HESTER [*astonished*]: Davey . . . [*She hurries to watch him leaving, to the right, halts.*] Why . . . he's running! [*Calling in alarm.*] Davey! [*She runs out.*]

J.B., PAT *and* DAN *stand, watching them open-mouthed as they disappear down the driveway.* AMOS *is center, downstage.*

DIBBLE: What in the world come over the boy? I didn't finish payin' him.

They stand looking right. AMOS *looks at the coat. He starts turning it inside out, examining it carefully, perplexed . . . Slow Curtain.*

ACT TWO

Scene i

June. Three years later. The living room of the FALKS'*—now* DAVID's*—house. A farmhouse room, but brightly done over. Solid door to outside at the right. In the back wall, right, a swinging door to the dining room. A stairway at the back, its landing at the left. A door, leading to an office in the bedroom, down left. One window at left. Two windows flanking the door to outside at right. Good blue rug, odd pieces, some new, some old. Oak. A pair of well-used rubber boots beside the door.*

The stage is empty. A perfect summer day, not too hot. Noon. After a moment the doorbell rings.

HESTER [*from above, shouts excitedly*]: They're here! Davey!

DAVID [*hurrying down the stairs, buttoning on a white shirt. He wears pressed pants, shined shoes, his hair has just been combed; shouting up*]: I'll get it, I'm going!

HESTER [*her head sticking out at the junction of banister and ceiling. She quickly surveys the room as* DAVID *comes off the stairs*]: Get your boots out of there! I just fixed up the house! *The bell rings.*

DAVID [*calling toward the door*]: Just a minute! [*getting the boots together. To* HESTER.] Go on, get dressed, it's almost noon! [*He opens door to dining room.*]

HESTER: Don't put them in there! They're filthy! Down the cellar!

DAVID: But I always put them in here!

HESTER: But you promised once the house is painted!

Door opens. Enter GUS.

GUS: Don't bother. It's only me.

He wears a white Palm Beach suit, hatless. HESTER *and* DAVID *stare at him in astonishment. She comes down the stairs. She is dressed in a robe, but has her best shoes on. Her hair is set.*

HESTER: Why, Gus! You look so handsome!

GUS: It is such a special day, I decided to make an impression on myself.

HESTER: No, you go perfectly with the room.

DAVID [*laughing with* GUS]: Watch yourself or she'll hang you in a frame over the couch. [*He stamps at her to get her moving.*]

HESTER [*squealing, she runs to the stairs and up a few steps, and leans over the banister*]: Is your girl outside? Bring her in.

DAVID: Hey, that's right! Where's your girl?

GUS [*looking up*]: Well, we both decided suddenly that until she can become as beautiful as Hester . . .

HESTER: Oh, you.

GUS [*opening his arms like a pleading lover*]: Until she shows ability to make over a house like this was, and until etcetera and etcetera, she is not the girl for me, so I haven't seen her all week. Anyway, I have decided definitely I need only a red-headed girl.

HESTER [*to* GUS]: Stand in the middle of the room when they come in. You make it look just like the picture in the *Ladies Home Journal*.

DAVID [*starting after her*]: Get dressed, will ya? Dad'll cut my head off if we're not ready!

HESTER *laughs with delight and runs upstairs.*

GUS [*looking around*]: It came out so nice. You know, this house shines in the sun a quarter of a mile away.

DAVID: Well, look at that sun! [*Goes right to windows.*] God must've pulled up the sun this morning, grabbed him by the back of the neck, and said—make it a baseball day.

GUS [*touching the wall*]: Now it is truly a place to call home. Amazing.

DAVID [*laughs musingly, indicating the windows at the right*]:

You know, when I came down this morning that window caught my eye. I used to sneak under that window when we were kids and peek in here to watch Hester doing her homework. And then I used to sneak away. And now I can walk in and outa this house fifty times a day and sleep up in his room night after night! [*Looks through the window.*] Wherever he is I bet he still can't figure it out. Read the encyclopedia if you like. I'll put on a tie. [*Goes to the landing.*]

GUS [*looking around*]: Encyclopedia, furniture, new plumbing. . . . When am I going to see a couple of brats around here!

DAVID [*stops at the landing*]: What's the rush, you got some old suits you want ruined?

GUS: Me? I always pick up babies by the back of the neck, but . . . [*Idly.*] without children you wouldn't have to fix nothin' in here for twenty years. When nothing breaks it's boring. [*He sits, reaches over for an encyclopedia volume.*]

DAVID [*glances above, comes away from stairs. Quietly*]: I been wanting to ask you about that.

GUS: What?

DAVID [*hesitates. In good humor*]: Did you ever hear of it happening when people didn't have kids because of the man?

GUS: Certainly, why not? Why don't you talk it over with her?

DAVID [*laughs self-consciously*]: I can't seem to get around to it. I mean we somehow always took it for granted, kinda, that when the time was right a kid would just naturally come along.

GUS: You go to the doctor, then you'll know. . . . Or do you want to know?

DAVID: Sure I do, but I don't know, it just doesn't seem *right*, especially when we've been all set financially for over two years now.

GUS: Right! What has this got to do with right or wrong? There is no justice in the world.

DAVID [*looks at him, then goes to the landing, stops*]: I'll never believe that, Gus. If one way or another a man don't receive according to what he deserves inside . . . well, it's a madhouse.

HESTER [*from above*]: There's a car stopping in front of the house! [*Coming down.*] Did you put your boots away?

DAVID [*slightly annoyed*]: Yeh, I put 'em away! [*Goes across to the door.*]

HESTER [*hurrying downstairs*]: You didn't! [*Hurrying across the room toward the boots.*] He'll have the place like a pigsty in a week!

DAVID *opens the door and looks out.*

GUS [*to* HESTER]: Get used to it, the place will never be so neat once you have children around.

DAVID *turns to him, quickly, resentment in his face.*

HESTER [*stops moving. An eager glow lights up her expression. The boots are in her hand*]: Don't you think it is a wonderful house for children?

DAVID: Hello! Hello, Mr. Dibble! Didn't expect to see you around here today. Come in, come in.

Enter DAN DIBBLE *after wiping his feet carefully on the doormat.*

DIBBLE: Had to see J.B. on some business. Thought I'd stop in, say hello. Afternoon, Mrs. Beeves.

HESTER: Hello, Mr. Dibble. [*She picks up the boots and goes out.*]

DAVID: You know Gus Eberson. He's with me over at the shop.

DIBBLE: Sure, how are you, Gus? Say, you look more like a banker than a mechanic.

DAVID: Best mechanic there is.

DIBBLE: What I always say—never judge a man by his clothes. A man and his clothes are soon parted. [*They laugh.*] Say, J.B. was tellin' me you used to have a shop of your own here in town—over in Poplar Street was it . . . ?

DAVID: We amalgamated, Gus and I.

GUS: Actually, Mr. Dibble, I ran out of money and customers after the first seven months. I am working now for Mr. Beeves since over two years.

DIBBLE: Well, say, this is the first time I knew a hired man to insist he wasn't the boss's partner, and the boss to let on he was.

GUS [*chuckles*]: Mr. Beeves suffers sometimes from an overdeveloped sense of responsibility.

DIBBLE: That's why I spotted him as a natural mink man. Given it any more thought, David?

DAVID: A lot, Mr. Dibble, a lot—but I'm afraid I haven't got an answer for you yet.

DIBBLE: Got time for a few facts today?

DAVID: Tell you the truth, we're expecting J.B. and Shory. Goin' up to Burley for the ball game. You heard about my brother, didn't you?

DIBBLE: J.B. said somethin' about him pitchin' against that colored team. Say, if he can knock them boys over he really belongs in the Big Leagues.

DAVID: I guess after today's game, Amos Beeves will be playin' for the Detroit Tigers.

DIBBLE: Well, say, they really took him, eh?

DAVID: Just about. A Tiger scout's goin' to be in the grand-stand today.

DIBBLE: Well, say, it's about time.

DAVID: Yep, things even up, I guess in the long run. Why don't you drop around tonight. Havin' a big barbecue after the game.

Enter HESTER *from the dining room.*

DIBBLE: Thanks, I'd like to but I got to get back and see my mink get fed on time and proper.

HESTER: David just never stops talkin' about mink. [*Sits.*] Have you still got that tiny one with the white spot on his head?

DAVID [*seeing* HESTER's *interest kindles a happy liveliness in him*]: Oh, that one's probably been in and out of a dozen New York night clubs by this time. [*They laugh.*]

HESTER [*disturbed—to* DIBBLE]: Oh, you didn't kill her?

DAVID [*to* GUS *and* HESTER]: That's the way you get about mink, they're like people, little nervous people.

DIBBLE: I call them my little bankers myself. Pour a dollar's worth of feed down their gullets and they'll return you forty percent; best little bankers in the world.

DAVID: Except when they fall, Mr. Dibble, except when they fall.

DIBBLE: Mink never fall!

DAVID: Oh, now, Mr. Dibble . . .

DIBBLE: They don't! It's their keepers fall down on them. When a feller goes broke tryin' to raise mink it's mainly because he's a careless man. From everything I've seen, David, you ain't that kind. You got a farm here clean as a hospital and mink needs a clean place. You're the first and only man I thought of when I decided to sell off some of my breeders when my doctor told me to ease up.

DAVID: I been askin' around lately, and everybody I talked to . . .

DIBBLE [*to* GUS *too*]: I'm glad you made the inquiries. It shows you're a careful man. And now I'll tell you my answer. Easiest thing in the world is to kill a mink. Mink'll die of a cold draught; they'll die of heart failure; indigestion can kill them, a cut lip, a bad tooth or sex trouble. And worse than that, the mink is a temperamental old woman. I wear an old brown canvas coat when I work around them. If I change that coat it might start them to eating their young. A big loud noise like thunder, or a heavy hailstorm comes and the mother's liable to pick up the litter, put 'em out in the open part of the cage, and then she'll go back into the nest box and close her eyes. As though they're out of danger if they're out of her sight. And when the storm's over you might have six or eight kits drowned to death out there. I've seen mink murder each other, I've seen them eat themselves to death and starve themselves to death, and I've seen them die of just plain worry. But! Not on my ranch! I'll show my records to anybody.

DAVID [*to* GUS]: There's a business, boy!

GUS: A business! That's a slot machine. What do you need with mink?

DAVID: Oh, there's a kick in it, Gus. When you send a load of skins to New York you know you *did* something, you . . .

GUS: Why, you didn't do something? [*Indicates right.*] A great big shop you built up, a tractor station, how nice you made this farm . . . ?

DAVID [*not too intensely; he enjoys this talk*]: Yeh, but is a thing really yours because your name is on it? Don't you have to feel you're smart enough, or strong enough, or something enough to have won it before it's really yours? You can't bluff a mink into staying alive. [*Turns to* DIBBLE.] I tell you, Mr. Dibble . . .

DIBBLE: Take your time. Think about it . . .

DAVID: Let me call you. I'll let you know.

DIBBLE: Oh, I'll bide my time. Just remember, in New York they murder people for a mink coat. Women sell their jewels for mink, they sell their . . . them New York women'll sell damn near anything for mink!

They laugh, as horns of two cars sound urgently outside.

DAVID [*to* DIBBLE]: This is my brother!

GUS [*as* DAVID *opens the door*]: Look, like two peacocks!

HESTER [*at the door, over her shoulder ecstatically to* DIBBLE]: They've waited so long!

DAVID [*exuberantly, backing from the door*]: Here he comes! Christy Matthewson the Second!

Enter AMOS *and* PATTERSON *followed by* J.B.

HESTER [*grabbing* AMOS*'s hand*]: How's your arm, Ame!

AMOS [*winds up and pitches*]: Wham!—He's out!

PAT [*throwing up his arms*]: God bless this day! [*Suddenly.*] I'm not waiting for anybody! [*Threatens to go out again.*]

J.B. [*to* HESTER]: Shory's waiting in the car! Let's go!

HESTER: Bring him in. Let's have a drink!

Nobody hears her.

DAVID: What're you lookin' so sad about, Dad! [*Suddenly hugs* PAT.]

HESTER: Get some whiskey, Dave!

PAT [*indignantly—he has broken from* DAVE]: You want to suffocate in here? Open the windows in this house! [*He rushes around throwing windows up.*]

DAVID [*laughing*]: We're going in a minute! Where's the telegram, Ame! [AMOS *opens his mouth but* PAT *cuts him off.*]

PAT [*busy with the windows*]: Let the day come in! What a day! What a year! What a nation!

HESTER [*rushing after* PAT]: Did you bring the telegram? [*She corners him, laughing.*] Where's the telegram?

PAT: I don't need to bring it. I will never forget that telegram so long as I live. [*Takes it out of his pocket.*] "Western Union. Class of Service. This is a full-rate Telegram or Cablegram unless its deferred character is indicated by a suitable symbol . . ."

HESTER: What're you reading that part for? [*Tries to grab it from him.*] What did the scout say!

PAT [*grabbing it back*]: I'm reading it to you just the way I read it when I got it—from the very top, to the very bottom.

DAVID: Let him read it, Hess!

They go quiet.

PAT: I haven't felt this way since the last time I read the Bible. "Patterson Beeves, 26 Murdock Street. Will be in Burley for the Black Giants game Sunday, July 16th. Looking forward to seeing Amos Beeves's performance. Best regards, Augie Belfast, Detroit Tigers." [*Looks around imperiously.*] Twenty-one years I have been waiting for this telegram. Training him down the cellar since he was old enough to walk. People laughed when Amos got bad marks in school. Forget the homework, I said. Keep your eye on the ball. Concentration, I said . . .

J.B. [*touched and fearing* PAT's *continuing indefinitely*]: For God's sake, let's all have a drink!

DAVID: Comin' up! [*Goes out door.*]

HESTER [*pointing outside. To* J.B.]: I'll bring Ellie in! Why don't you come to the game with us, Mr. Dibble? [*She starts across to the door.*]

J.B. [*a little embarrassed, stops* HESTER]: Better leave her, baby. You know how she is about alcohol. Let's not start anything.

GUS: Shory likes a drink. I'll bring him in. [*He goes out left.*]

PAT: Plenty of room in Dave's car, Mr. Dibble. [*He studies* DIBBLE, *automatically massaging* AMOS's *arm.*]

J.B. [*holds his hand out to* HESTER]: What do you think of this?

HESTER: A wedding ring! You're giving Ellie a new ring?

J.B. [*warmly*]: No, this is for me. Since we decided to adopt a baby I been feeling like we're newlyweds.

HESTER [*flings her arms around him*]: You're such a silly man! *Enter* SHORY, *pushed in by* GUS.

SHORY [*to* J.B.]: Hey, Poppa, don't start nothin' you can't finish.

Enter DAVID *with drinks on a tray.*

HESTER [*three-quarters joking, but only that much. To* SHORY]: And you've got a filthy mind.

SHORY: Madam, don't flatter me. [*To* DAVID, *who has been watching* HESTER *since* SHORY *came in.*] Hey, husband, where's that drink?

DAVID: Come on, everybody. Before we go! [*Gives out the drinks. . . . Raises his glass.*] A toast! To everybody's luck— everybody's!

All raise their glasses.

GUS [*to* AMOS]: And the next World Series! [*Starts to drink.*]

DAVID: Wait! Make one big toast . . . to all our hearts' desires. For Amos! For Dad . . .

GUS: To David and Hester! To their prosperity, their shop, their tractor station, their farm . . .

DIBBLE [*suddenly struck with the idea*]: And their mink!

HESTER [*quick complaint*]: No . . .

DAVID [*he looks at* HESTER. *Her face softens toward him*]: Not the mink now! From today on everything is coming true! To our children.

GUS: To their children.

J.B.: Their children.

HESTER [*softly*]: And in this year. Say that.

DAVID [*their eyes meet for an instant, and hold*]: In this year . . . everything our hearts desire . . . *all of us*: in this year.

All drink.

PAT [*looks at watch*]: Hey! We're late! We're getting drunk and the whole world is waiting for us out there! Come on!

They all rush out yelling and laughing as . . .

Curtain.

Scene ii

Living Room. About seven o'clock that night.

The stage is empty. The gentle murmur and occasional laughter of the guests at the barbecue can be heard dimly.

Presently, DAVID, *followed by* DAN DIBBLE, *comes in through the front door.* DAVID *crosses to the desk and removes a large checkbook. He pauses over it, pen in hand.*

DAVID: It's a fortune. I never wrote a check this big in my life.

DIBBLE: You never got so much for so little, David. You'll have prize stock, the finest breeding mink alive. The rest's up to you.

DAVID: Mr. Dibble, I never thought I'd see my hand shaking. *The door at lower left opens and* PAT *appears. He closes the door gently behind him.*

DAVID: Still asleep?

PAT: Shhh, I always make him take a long nap after a game.

DAVID: Aren't you going to eat anything?

PAT: I couldn't eat anything now. I'll eat after Belfast gets here. [*He sits on the couch.*] I was watchin' Amos just now asleep on the couch, and it suddenly struck me. Did you ever notice what a powerful face he has?

DAVID [*as he writes check*]: He's great. After that game today there ain't a man in the world can doubt it. He's just great.

PAT: Didn't he look noble out there?

DAVID: Noble enough to vote for.

DAVID [*as he tears out check*]: Here's your check, Mr. Dibble. [DIBBLE *takes it.*]

DIBBLE: You'll never regret it, David.

DAVID: I hope not.

DIBBLE: Well, I'll be runnin' along now. You call me as soon as you get your cages ready and I'll bring 'em over. [DAVID *has walked him to the front door.*] Goodnight.

DAVID: G'night.

DIBBLE *exits.* DAVID *turns back into the room.*

PAT: You know why I'm extra glad? I think you were beginning to take it too hard, Dave. I was going to have a talk with you. Because I never had a doubt he'd scale the heights.

DAVID: I just didn't like the idea of me getting everything so steady, and him waiting around like . . . I mean you get to wondering if your own turn isn't coming.

PAT: Like what do you mean?

DAVID: A loss . . . a big unhappiness of some kind. But he's on his way now. I know it, Pop.

The door opens and J.B. *enters with a grand new valise. He is slightly drunk. In one hand he has a slip of paper.*

J.B.: Surprise! [PAT *springs up with finger to his lips.*]

PAT: Shhh!

J.B. [*whispers*]: Surprise! Wake him up. [*Pointing to valise.*] Surprise . . .

PAT: After a game he's got to sleep an hour or he's peevish. [*Pointing at watch.*] Wait a few minutes.

DAVID: Wait'll he sees the initials.

PAT [*violently*]: Ssh! [*To* J.B. . . . *threatening.*] If he's peevish . . . !

The door opens and AMOS *stands in the doorway.*

J.B.: Hey Amos . . . [*Holding up valise.*] Surprise.

AMOS: Aw . . . ! [AMOS *takes the valise and fingers it happily.*]

J.B.: It's a token of our affection from . . . just a minute now . . . [*Straightens the slip of paper.*] Hester, Shory, Gus, Dave, Ellie, and me, and Belle. [*Indicating upstage.*]

AMOS [*fondling the valise*]: Gee, you should'na done it.

J.B. [*with growing flourish and sentiment*]: No, you don't realize the traveling you'll do. [*Looks into the distance.*] Shibe Park, Commiskey Field, Sportsman's Park—Boston, Chicago, Cleveland, St. Louis. . . . And when you're packing up after a nice no-hitter, you'll give us a thought in the old home town. [*To clinch it, he taps a buckle.*] Solid brass.

AMOS [*feverish in glory*]: Give me that list. [*Takes it out of* J.B.'s *hand.*] When I get my first paycheck I'm gonna send you all a big present! Say . . . ! [*Starting to take* PAT's *wrist to look at his watch.*] What time . . . ?

PAT [*holding onto his arm*]: You heard what he said in the locker room. He's got to finish some long-distance phoning, and then he'll be here. Come on. I'll rub you down.

HESTER *enters as they start for the stairs.*

HESTER: John, you better go outside. Ellie's going home.

J.B. [*frightened and hurt*]: Why? [*To all.*] Am I so drunk?

DAVID: Hurry up, maybe you can catch her.

J.B.: Come with me, Dave . . . tell her . . .

DAVID: Get washed, Ame . . . you want to look nice now. Be right back.

DAVID *and* J.B. *go out.*

HESTER [*looking at the door*]: Why must he always do that? [*To* PAT *who is rummaging in his old valise.*] I'll get you some towels. Come on up.

PAT: Oh, no, we carry our own. You never can tell about strange towels. [*He folds one over his arm.* AMOS *is looking out of the window.*]

HESTER [*ready to laugh*]: Well, I wasn't going to give you a dirty towel, you stupid.

PAT: For twenty-one years I've kept him practically sterilized. I ain't layin' him low with an infection now. Come on, Amos, get washed.

AMOS *and* PAT *exit up the stairs as* J.B. *enters, followed by* DAVID. J.B. *is drunk, unsteady but not staggering. He barges in, comes directly to* HESTER *and takes her hand, speaks very close to her face, as though to discern her reactions better.*

J.B.: Hester, you got to go home for me. [*He goes to window helplessly.*]

DAVID: Maybe she was only fooling, John . . .

J.B.: No! But . . . [*To* HESTER.] Somebody's got to go home for me! [*And suddenly he bursts into uncontrolled sobbings.*]

HESTER: What in the world . . . !

DAVID [*angrily*]: John! [*Shakes him, then seats him.*] John! Are you going to cut that out?

HESTER [*going to* J.B.]: What happened? What did she say?

J.B. [*stops sobbing, sits swaying backward and forward, very slightly in his chair*]: All these years . . . we could've had children . . . all these weary, weary years.

HESTER: What are you talking about?

J.B. [*pointing waywardly toward the door to the outside*]: Just told me . . . she made it up about the doctor . . . made it all up. We could've had two kids by now. [*Looks at* DAVID.] She wouldn't. She wouldn't. Because I drink, she says. A drunkard, she says! They'll wipe my name off my mail box like I never lived!

HESTER: Come upstairs and lie down. You make me so mad I could choke you! You could have everything in the world and you drink it away.

J.B.: If I had a boy . . . I wouldn't have touched a drop.

HESTER: Oh, push! [*She tries to move him to the stairway.*]

J.B.: I'm only a failure, Dave. The world is full of failures. All a man needs is one mistake and he's a failure.

DAVID *turns his head, a little annoyed.*

DAVID [*impatiently*]: I know, John. [*Looks out window again.*]

J.B.: You are the only man I ever knew who never makes a mistake. You understand me. Look at me! I am saying something.

DAVID [*now turns full to him*]: What are you talking about?

J.B.: I'm not as drunk as I look, David! You're a good man, yes. You know how to do. But you've had a phenomenal lot of luck in your life, Dave. Never play luck too hard. It's like a season, and seasons go away.

HESTER: Come up or you'll pass away.

Enter PAT *downstairs with watch in hand.*

PAT: My watch says eight-thirty, where is he? He told you no later than eight o'clock, didn't he?

DAVID: Which means he's half an hour late. That's what it means, doesn't it?

PAT: I don't know what to tell Amos. I made him take another shower.

DAVID [*with growing fear*]: He pitched the greatest game of his life today, what more does he need to be told? That man'll be here.

PAT: Maybe he was kidding us. He looked like he might be that type.

DAVID: Are you going to stop that?

PAT: . . . And Amos did look a little nervous in the eighth inning with those two men on base.

DAVID: But they didn't score! Now will you just stop. [PAT, *hurt looks at him, then goes to the stairs.*] Dad, what you want me to do; I can't grow him in my back yard, can I?

SHORY *enters pushed by* GUS. *At the stairs,* PAT *turns, starts to speak, then goes up and out.*

SHORY [*as the door shuts*]: I'm getting my aches and pains. I
   came in to say goodnight. . . . Party's breakin' up anyway
   out there.

DAVID: No, wait a little. I don't want everybody pulling out.
   [*He goes to window as . . .*]

SHORY: The man told you seven-thirty, what're you making
   believe he said eight? You told me as he said seven-thirty,
   didn't you?

DAVID [*his fury is at the scout. He keeps searching out of the
   window*]: He could've got a flat maybe.

SHORY: It don't take an hour to change a flat, Dave.

DAVID [*tensely. He turns*]: Don't go away. Please.
   Enter HESTER.
       [*To* HESTER.] The folks are starting to go. [*Moving her
   back to the door.*] I want a party here when the scout leaves.
   Keep them here.

HESTER: It's not the world coming to an end. I don't want you
   acting this way. It's no fault of yours what happens to him.
   [*She grasps him.*] Why do you act this way? Davey . . .

DAVID: I don't get it, I swear to God I don't get it. [*Strides to
   the window. He seems about to burst from the room.*]

SHORY: Get what?

DAVID: Everything is so hard for him. [*Turns to them suddenly,
   unable to down his anxiety.*] I want to ask you something.
   All of you, and you too, Hess. You know what I can do and
   what I can't do, you . . . you know me. Everything I touch,
   why is it? It turns gold. Everything.

HESTER: What's come over you? Why . . . ?

DAVID [*with extreme urgency*]: It bothers me, it . . . [*To all.*]
   What is it about me? I never . . . I never lose. Since we were
   kids I expected Amos to rise and shine. He's the one, he
   knows something, he knows one thing perfect. Why? Is it all
   luck? Is that what it is?

GUS: Nonsense. You're a good man, David.

DAVID: Aren't you good?

GUS: Yes, but I . . .

DAVID: Then why did your shop fail? Why are you working for
   me now? [*He moves as one in the throes of release.*]

GUS: They remember the war here, Dave, they don't like to buy from a foreigner.

DAVID: No, that's crazy.

GUS: Also, I had a second-rate location.

DAVID: Gus, it was better than mine. Every car coming into town had to pass your place. And they came to me. Why is that?

GUS: You know an engine, Dave, you . . .

DAVID: Including Marmons? [*To all.*] I got fourteen thousand dollars in the bank and as much again standing on the ground. Amos? Never had a nickel. Not a bloody nickel. Why?
A slight pause.

HESTER [*goes to him. Smiles to make him smile but he does not*]: Why does it bother you? It's good to be lucky. Isn't it?

DAVID [*looks at her a moment*]: Isn't it better to feel that what you have came to you because of something special you can do? Something, something . . . inside you? Don't you have to know what that thing is?

HESTER: Don't you know?

DAVID: . . . I don't, I don't know.

SHORY: And you'll never know . . .

DAVID: Damn it all, if everything drops on you like fruit from a tree, for no reason, why can't it break away for no reason? Everything you have . . . suddenly.

HESTER [*takes DAVID's arm*]: Come, say goodbye to the folks.

DAVID: No . . . they're not going home till the scout comes! Now go out . . .

HESTER [*shakes his arm*]: It's his hard luck, not yours!

DAVID: It is mine! A man has a right to get what he deserves. He does, damn it! [*He goes to the window, breaking from her.*]

HESTER [*angrily*]: You talk like you'd stole something from him. You never got anything you didn't deserve. You . . .

DAVID [*at the end of his patience, he turns on her*]: Am I that good and he that bad? I can't believe it. There's something wrong, there's something wrong! [*Suddenly.*] I'm going to Burley. [*To HESTER, hurriedly.*] Where's the keys to the car . . . ?

HESTER: You don't even know where to find the man . . .

DAVID: I'll find him, where are the keys?

HESTER [*she grabs him*]: Davey, stop it . . .

DAVID: I'm going, I'll drag him here . . . !

HESTER [*frightened*]: Davey . . . !

He strides toward the door. SHORY *grabs his arm and holds it fast.*

SHORY: Stop it!

DAVID: Let go of me!

SHORY [*he will not let go*]: Listen to me, you damn fool! There's nothing you can do, you understand?

DAVID: Let go of my arm . . .

SHORY [*forces him down into a chair*]: David, I'm going to tell you something . . . I never told you before. But you need to know this now. Amos deserves better than this, but I deserved better than this too. [*Pats his thighs.*] When I went to France there was no broken bones in my imagination. I left this town with a beautiful moustache and full head of hair. Women traveled half the state to climb into my bed. Even over there, under shot and shell, as they say, there was a special star over my head. I was the guy nothin' was ever going to hit . . . And nothin' ever did, David. [*He releases* DAVID's *arm. Now* DAVID *does not move away.*] Right through the war without a scratch. Surprised? I walked into Paris combing my hair. The women were smiling at me from both sides of the street, and I walked up the stairs with the whistles blowing out the Armistice. I remember how she took off my shoes and put them under the bed. The next thing I knew the house was laying on my chest and they were digging me out. DAVID, *all, stare at him.*

HESTER: Everybody said it was a battle, I thought . . .

SHORY [*to her*]: No, no battle at all. [*To* DAVID.] In battle— there's almost a reason for it, a man almost "deserves" it that way. I just happened to pick out the one woman in Paris who lived in a house where the janitor was out getting drunk on the Armistice. He forgot to put water in the furnace boiler. [*Smiles.*] The walls blew out. [*Points upstage with his thumb over his shoulder.*] Amos's walls happened to blow out. And you happen to be a lucky boy, brother David. A jellyfish can't swim no matter how he tries; it's the tide that pushes him every time. So just keep feeding, and enjoy the water till you're thrown up on the beach to dry.

Pause.

HESTER [*goes to him*]: Come, Dave, the folks are waiting to say goodbye.

DAVID *is forced to turn quickly toward the window. It is an indecisive turn of the head, a questioning turn, and she follows as he strides to the window and looks out toward upstage direction . . .*

DAVID: Wait! [*Starting for the window.*] A car? [*Turns quickly to them all.*] It didn't go past. It stopped. [*He starts quickly for the door, across the stage, right.* PAT *rushes down the stairs.*]

PAT: He's here! He came! Get out, everybody! [*To all.*] All the way from Burley in a taxicab! Dave, you stay. I want your advice when he starts talkin' contract! [PAT *rushes out.*]

DAVID [*as they all keep exclaiming*]: Out, out, all of you! [*As they start for door,* DAVID *musses* SHORY.] Where's your jellyfish now, brother!

SHORY [*at door with the others*]: His luck is with him, sister, that's all, his luck!

DAVID: Luck, heh? [*Smiling, he bends over* SHORY, *pointing left toward his big desk and speaking privately . . .*] Some day remind me to open the middle drawer of that desk. I'll show you a fistful of phone bills for calls to Detroit.

GUS [*joyously*]: Dave. You called them!

DAVID: Sure, I called them. That man is here because I brought him here! [*To* SHORY.] Where's the jellyfish could've done that! [*Triumphantly, to all.*] Don't anybody go. We're going to raise the roof tonight!

They have all gone out now, on his last lines. Only HESTER *remains in the doorway.*

DAVID *looks at her a moment, and with a laugh embraces her quickly.*

I'll tell you everything he says.

HESTER: Be like this all the time, Davey. [*She turns toward the hallway into which this door leads.*] Tell me every word, now. [*She goes.*]

DAVID *quickly brushes his hair back, looking rapidly about the room and to himself* . . .

DAVID: Now it's wonderful: This is how it ought to be!

Enter AMOS—*comes down stairs.*

AMOS [*hushed, with his hands clasped as though in prayer*]: God, it's happening just like it ought've. 'Cause I'm good. I betcha I'm probably great! [*He says this, facing the door, glancing at* DAVID.]

Enter AUGIE BELFAST *and* PAT. AUGIE *is a big Irishman dressed nattily.*

PAT [*as they enter*]: . . . couldn't stop him from setting up a party. [*Sees* DAVE.] Oh, here he is.

AUGIE [*to* AMOS *and* DAVID.]: Sit down, sit down. Don't stand on ceremony with me. I'm Augie Belfast . . .

AMOS *sits on the couch.* DAVID *in a chair. As* PAT . . .

PAT: Let me have your coat?

AUGIE [*lays down his hat*]: It don't bother me. I live in it. Thanks just the same. [*Taking out chewing gum.*] Gum?

DAVID: No thanks, we've been eating all day.

AUGIE [*unfolding a slice as* PAT *sits. He moves about constantly; he already has a wad of gum in his cheek*]: Loosen up, don't stand in awe of me. [*To* DAVID *and* AMOS.] I was just telling your father . . . I got tied up in Burley on some long-distance calls. I'm very sorry to be so late. [*He is anxious to be pardoned.*]

DAVID: Oh, that's all right. We know how busy you fellas are.

AUGIE: Thanks. I knew how you must've been feeling. [*He paces a little, chewing, looking at the floor.*] Amos? [*He says nothing for a long moment. Stops walking, looks down, slowly unfolds another slice of gum.*]

AMOS [*whisper*]: Ya?

AUGIE: Amos, how long you been pitchin'?

AMOS: Well, about . . . [*Turns to* PAT.]

PAT: Steadily since he's been nine years old.

AUGIE [*nods. Pause*]: I guess you know he's a damn fine pitcher.

PAT [*comfortably*]: We like to think so around here.

AUGIE: Yeh, he's steady, he's good. Got a nice long arm, no

nerves in that arm. He's all right. He feels the plate. [*All the time thinking of something else, pacing.*]

PAT: Well, you see, I've had him practicing down the cellar against a target. Dug the cellar out deeper so he could have room after he grew so tall.

AUGIE: Yeh, I know. Man sitting next to me this afternoon was telling me. Look, Mr. Beeves . . . [*He straddles a chair, folds his arms on its back, facing them.*] I want you to have confidence in what I say. I'm Augie Belfast, if you know anything about Augie Belfast you know he don't bull. There's enough heartbreak in this business without bull-throwers causin' any more. *In toto,* I don't string an athlete along. Pitchin' a baseball to me is like playin' the piano well, or writin' beautiful literature, so try to feel I'm giving you the last word because I am. [PAT *nods a little, hardly breathing.*] I have watched many thousands of boys, Mr. Beeves. I been whackin' the bushes for material for a long time. You done a fine job on Amos. He's got a fine, fast ball, he's got a curve that breaks off sharp, he's got his control down to a pinpoint. He's almost original sometimes. When it comes to throwin' a ball, he's all there. Now. [*Slight pause.*] When I saw him two years ago, I said . . .

DAVID [*electrically*]: You were *here* before?

AUGIE: Oh yeh, I meant to tell you. I came to see him last year, too . . .

PAT: Why didn't you let me know?

AUGIE: Because there was one thing I couldn't understand, Mr. Beeves. I understand it today, but I couldn't then. When the bases are clear, Mr. Beeves, and there's nobody on, your boy is terrific. . . . Now wait a minute, let me say rather that he's good, very good. . . . I don't want to say an untruth, your boy is good when nobody's on. But as soon as a man gets on base and starts rubbin' his spikes in the dirt and makin' noise behind your boy's back, something happens to him. I seen it once, I seen it twice. I seen it every time the bases get loaded. And once the crowd starts howlin', your body, Mr. Beeves, is floatin' somewhere out in paradise.

PAT: But he pitched a shut-out.

AUGIE: Only because them Black Giants like to swing bats. If they'd waited him out in the eighth inning they could've walked in half a dozen runs. You boy was out of control. [*Dead silence.*] I couldn't understand it. I absolutely couldn't get the angle on it. Here's a boy with a terrific. . . . Well, let's not say terrific, let's say a damn good long arm. But not an ounce of base-brains. There is something in him that prevents him from playin' the bases . . .

PAT: I know, I've been drilling him the last three years.

AUGIE: I know, but in three years there's been no improvement. In fact, this year he's worse in that respect than last year. Why? Today I found the answer.

PAT [*softly*]: You did?

AUGIE: The guy sitting next to me mentions about him pitchin' down the cellar since he was nine years old. That was it! Follow me now. In the cellar there is no crowd. In the cellar he knows exactly what's behind his back. In the cellar, *in toto,* your boy is home. He's only got to concentrate on that target, his mind is trained to take in that one object, just the target. But once he gets out on a wide ball field, and a crowd is yelling in his ears, and there's two or three men on bases jumpin' back and forth behind him, his mind has got to do a lot of things at once, he's in a strange place, he gets panicky, he gets paralyzed, he gets mad at the base runners and he's through! From that minute he can't pitch worth a nickel bag of cold peanuts!

He gets up, pulls down his vest. DAVID *and* PAT *sit dumbly,* AMOS *staring at nothing.*

   I got to make a train, Mr. Beeves.

PAT [*slowly rises. As though in a dream*]: I didn't want to waste the winters, that's why I trained him down the cellar.

AUGIE [*thoughtfully*]: Yeh, that's just where you made your mistake, Mr. Beeves.

DAVID [*rises*]: But . . . that was his plan. He didn't want to waste the winters. Down the cellar . . . it seemed like such a good idea!

AUGIE: But it was a mistake.

DAVID: But he's been doing it twelve years! A man can't be multiplying the same mistake for twelve years, can he?

AUGIE: I guess he can, son. It was a very big mistake.

Pause.

PAT: Well . . . you can't take that out of him? Your coaches and . . . everything?

AUGIE: There's no coach in the world can take out a boy's brain and set it back twelve years. Your boy is crippled up here. [*Taps his temple.*] I'm convinced.

DAVID: But if you coached him right, if you drilled him day after day . . .

AUGIE: It would take a long, long time, and I personally don't believe he'll ever get rid of it.

PAT: You can't . . . you can't try him, eh?

AUGIE: I know how you feel, Mr. Beeves, but I am one man who will not take a boy out of his life when I know in my heart we're going to throw him away like a wet rag.

DAVID [*for a long time he stands staring*]: He has no life.

AUGIE [*bends closer to hear*]: Eh?

DAVID: He doesn't know how to do anything else.

AUGIE [*nods with sympathy*]: That was another mistake. [*He starts to turn away to go.*]

PAT [*as though to call him back somehow*]: I believed if he concentrated . . . concentration . . . you see I myself always jumped from one thing to another and never got anywhere, and I thought . . .

AUGIE: Yeh . . . when it works concentration is a very sound principle. [*Takes a breath.*] Well, lots of luck.

Still unable to believe, PAT *can't speak.*

'Bye, Amos.

AMOS *nods slightly, numbly staring. At the door, to* DAVE.

'Bye. [*He starts to open the door.*]

DAVID: Look . . . [*He hurries to him. He looks in his eyes, his hand raised as though to grab the man and hold him here.*]

AUGIE: Yeh?

DAVID *starts to speak, then looks at* AMOS *who is still staring at nothing.* DAVID *turns back to* AUGIE.

DAVID: . . . You'll see him in the Leagues.

AUGIE: I hope so. I just don't . . .

DAVID [*trying to restrain his fury*]: No, you'll see him. You're
not the only team, you know. You'll see him in the Leagues.

AUGIE [*grasps* DAVID*'s arm*]: . . . Take it easy, boy. [*To the
others.*] I hope you'll pardon me for being late.

DAVID [*quietly, like an echo, his voice cracking*]: You'll see
him.

AUGIE *nods. Glances at* PAT *and* AMOS, *opens the door and
goes.* PAT *and* DAVID *stand looking at the door.* PAT *turns
now, walks slowly to* AMOS *who is sitting. As* PAT *nears him
he stand slowly, his fists clenched at his sides.*

PAT [*softly, really questioning*]: He can be wrong too, can't he?
[AMOS *is silent, his face filling with hate.*] Can't he be wrong?
[*No reply.*] He can, can't he?

AMOS [*a whip-like shout*]: No, he can't be!

PAT: But everybody makes mistakes . . .

AMOS [*with a cry he grabs* PAT *by the collar and shakes him
violently back and forth*]: Mistakes! Mistakes! You and your
goddam mistakes!

DAVID [*leaps to them, trying to break his grip*]: Let him go!
Amos, let him go!

AMOS [*amid his own, and* PAT*'s weeping. To* PAT]: You liar! I'll
kill you, you little liar, *you liar!*
With a new burst of violence he starts forcing PAT *backward
and down to the floor.* GUS *comes in as* DAVID *locks an arm
around* AMOS*'s neck and jerks him from* PAT *who falls to the
floor.*

     Leave me alone! Leave me alone!
With a great thrust DAVID *throws* AMOS *to the couch and
stands over him, fists raised.*

DAVID: Stay there! Don't get up! You'll fight me, Amos!

PAT [*scurrying to his feet, and taking* DAVID *away from the
couch*]: Don't, don't fight! [*He turns quickly, pleadingly to*
AMOS, *who is beginning to sob on the couch.*] Amos, boy,
boy . . . [AMOS *lies across the couch and sobs violently.* PAT
leans over and pats his head.] Boy, boy . . .

AMOS *swings his arm out blindly and hits* PAT *across the chest.* DAVID *starts toward them but* PAT *remains over him, patting his back.*

Come on, boy, please, boy, stop now, stop, Amos! Look, Ame, look, I'll get Cleveland down here, I'll go myself, I'll bring a man. Ame, listen, I did what I could, a man makes mistakes, he can't figure on everything. . . . [*He begins shaking* AMOS *who continues sobbing.*] Ame, stop it! [*He stands and begins shouting over* AMOS'S *sobbing.*] I admit it, I admit it, Ame, I lie, I talk too much, I'm a fool, I admit it, but look how you pitch, give me credit for that, give me credit for something! [*Rushes at* AMOS *and turns him over.*] Stop that crying! God Almighty, what do you want me to do! I'm a fool, what can I do!

DAVID [*wrenches* PAT *away from the couch. Stands over* AMOS]: Listen, you! [*Leans over and pulls* AMOS *by the collar to a sitting position.* AMOS *sits limply, sobbing.*] He made a mistake. That's over with. You're going to drill on base play. You got a whole life. One mistake can't ruin a life. He'll go to Cleveland. I'll send him to New York . . .

HESTER *enters quietly.*

The man can be wrong. Look at me! The man can be wrong, you understand!

AMOS *shakes his head.*

AMOS: He's right.

DAVID *releases him and stands looking down at him.* AMOS *gets up slowly, goes to a chair and sits.*

He's right. I always knew I couldn't play the bases. Everything the man said was right. I'm dumb, that's why. I can't figure nothin'. [*Looks up at* PAT.] There wasn't no time, he said, no time for nothin' but throwin' that ball. Let 'em laugh, he said, you don't need to know how to figure. He knew it all. He knows everything! Well, this is one time I know something. I ain't gonna touch a baseball again as long as I live!

PAT [*frantically*]: Amos, you don't know what you're saying . . . !

AMOS: I couldn't ever stand out on a diamond again! I can't do it! I know! I can't! [*Slight pause.*] I ain't goin' to let you kid me anymore. I'm through. [*He rises.* PAT *sobs into his hands.*]

DAVID [AMOS *keeps shaking his head in denial of everything*]: What do you mean, through? Amos, you can't lay down. Listen to me. Stop shaking your head—who gets what he wants in this world!

AMOS [*suddenly.*]: You. Only you.

DAVID: Me! Don't believe it, Amos. [*Grabs him.*] Don't believe that anymore!

AMOS: Everything you ever wanted . . . in your whole life, every . . . !

DAVID: Including my children, Ame? [*Silence.*] Where are my children?

HESTER: Dave . . .

DAVID [*to* HESTER]: I want to tell him! [*To* AMOS.] What good is everything when nothing is good without children? Do you know the laughingstock it makes of everything you do in the world? You'll never meet a man who doesn't carry one curse . . . at least one. Shory, J.B., Pop, you, and me too. Me as much as anybody!

HESTER: Don't, Davey . . .

DAVID [*with a dreadful triumph*]: No, Hess, I'm not afraid of it anymore. I want it out. I was always afraid I was something special in the world. But not after this. [*To* AMOS.] *Nobody* escapes, Ame! But I don't lay down, I don't die because I'll have no kids. A man is born with one curse at least to be cracked over his head. I see it now, and you got to see it. Don't envy me, Ame . . . we're the same now. The world is made that way, as if a law was written in the sky somewhere—nobody escapes! [*Takes* AMOS'*s hand.*]

HESTER [*almost weeping she cannot restrain*]: Why do you talk that way?

DAVID: Hess, the truth . . .

HESTER: It's not the truth! . . . You have no curse! None at all!

DAVID [*struck*]: What . . . ?

HESTER: I wanted to wait till the scout signed him up. And then . . . when the house was full of noise and cheering, I'd stand with you on the stairs high over them all, and tell them you were going to have a child. [*With anger and disappointment and grief.*] Oh Davey, I saw you so proud . . . !

DAVID [*twisted and wracked, he bursts out*]: Oh, Hess, I am, I am.

HESTER: No, you don't want it. I don't know what's happened to you, you don't want it now!

DAVID [*with a chill of horror freezing him*]: Don't say that! Hester, you mustn't . . . [DAVID *tries to draw her to him.*]

HESTER [*holding him away*]: You've got to want it, Davey. You've just got to want it!

She bursts into tears and rushes out. He starts after her, calling her name . . . when he finds himself facing AMOS.

AMOS: Nobody escapes . . . [DAVID *stops, turns to* AMOS.] . . . except you. [*He walks to the door, past* DAVID, *and goes out.*]

Curtain.

ACT THREE

Scene i

Living room. Night in the following February.

J.B. *is asleep on the couch.* SHORY *and* GUS *are silently play-ing cards and smoking at a table near the fireplace. Snow can be seen on the window muntins. Several coats on the rack. Presently . . .*

GUS: There's no brainwork in this game. Let me teach you claviash.
SHORY: I can win all the money I need in rummy and pinochle. Play.
GUS: You have no intellectual curiosity.
SHORY: No, but you can slip me a quarter. [*Showing his hand.*] Rummy.
Enter BELLE *from the stairs.*
GUS [*to* BELLE]: Everything all right?
BELLE [*half turns to him, holding blanket forth*]: She keeps sweating up all the blankets. That poor girl.
GUS: The doctor says anything?
BELLE: Yes . . . [*Thinks.*] . . . he said, go down and get a dry blanket.
GUS: I mean, about when it will be coming along?
BELLE: Oh, you can't tell about a baby. That's one thing about them, they come most any time. Sometimes when you don't expect it, and sometimes when you do expect it. [*She goes up to door and turns again.*] Why don't Davey buy a baby car-riage?

GUS: Didn't he? I suppose he will.

BELLE: But how can you have a baby without a baby carriage?

SHORY: You better blow your nose.

BELLE: I haven't time! [*She blows her nose and goes out, up left.*]

SHORY: A quarter says it's a boy. [*Tosses a quarter on the table.*]

GUS: It's a bet. You know, statistics show more girls is born than boys. You should've asked me for odds.

SHORY: Dave Beeves doesn't need statistics, he wants a boy. Matter of fact, let's raise it—a dollar to your half that he's got a boy tonight.

GUS: Statistically I would take the bet, but financially I stand pat. *Enter* DAVID *from left door to outside. He is dressed for winter. It is immediately evident that a deep enthusiasm, a ruddy satisfaction is upon him. He wears a strong smile. He stamps his feet a little as he removes his gloves, and then his short coat, muffler, hat, leaving a sweater on. As he closes the door.*

DAVID: How'm I doing upstairs?

GUS: So far she only sweats.

DAVID: Sweating! Is that normal?

GUS: Listen, she ain't up there eating ice cream.

DAVID [*goes to the fireplace, rubs his hands before it. Of* J.B. *as though amused*]: The least little thing happens and he stays home from work. He's been here all day.

GUS: Certain men like to make holidays. A new kid to him is always a holiday.

DAVID [*he looks around*]: What a fuss.

GUS: You're very calm. Surprising to me. Don't you feel nervous?

SHORY [*to Gus*]: You seen too many movies. What's the use of him pacing up and down?

DAVID [*with an edge of guilt*]: I got the best doctor; everything she needs. I figure, whatever's going to happen'll happen. After all, I can't . . .

Breaks off. In a moment BELLE *enters from the left door, carrying a different blanket. She goes toward the stair landing.* DAVID *finally speaks, unable to restrain it.*

Belle . . . [*She stops. He goes to her, restraining anxiety.*]

Would you ask the doctor . . . if he thinks it's going to be very hard for her, heh?

BELLE: He told me to shut up.

DAVID: Then ask J.B.'s wife.

BELLE: She told me to shut up too. But I'll ask her.

BELLE *goes up the stairs.* DAVID *watches her ascend a moment.*

DAVID [*looking upstairs*]: That girl is going to live like a queen after this. [*Turns to them, banging his fist in his palm.*] Going to make a lot of money this year.

SHORY: Never predict nothin' but the weather, half an hour ahead.

DAVID: Not this time. I just finished mating my mink, and I think every one of them took.

GUS: All finished? That's fine.

A knock is heard on the door. DAVID *goes to it, opens it.* PAT *enters. He is dressed in a pea jacket, a wool stocking cap on his head. He carries a duffle bag on his shoulder.*

DAVID: Oh, hello, Dad.

PAT: The baby come yet?

DAVID: Not yet.

PAT: My train doesn't leave for a couple of hours. I thought I'd wait over here.

DAVID: Here, give me that. [*He takes the duffle bag from* PAT, *puts it out of the way.*]

SHORY: So you're really going, Pat?

PAT: I got my old job back—ship's cook. I figure with a little studying, maybe in a year or so, I'll have my Third license. So . . .

DAVID: It's so foolish your leaving, Dad. Can't I change your mind?

PAT: It's better this way, David. Maybe if I'm not around Amos'll take hold of himself.

There is a knock on the door.

DAVID: That's probably Amos now.

He goes to the door, opens it. AMOS *enters. He is smoking a cigarette.*

Hello, Ame. All locked up? Come in.

AMOS: I got my motor running. Hello, Gus, Shory. [*He ignores* PAT. *There is a pause.*]

GUS: Working hard?

AMOS [*a tired, embittered chuckle*]: Yeh, pretty tough; pumpin' gas, ringin' the cash register . . . [*Giving* DAVID *a small envelope and a key.*] There's twenty-six bucks in there. I got the tally slip in with it.

DAVID [*as though anxious for his participation; strained*]: Twenty-six! We did all right today.

AMOS: Always do, don't ya? 'Night. [*Starts to go.*]

DAVID: Listen, Ame. [AMOS *turns.*] The mink'll be bearing in about a month. I was thinking you might like to take a shot at working with me, here . . . it's a great exercise. . . . Spring is coming, you know. You want to be in condition . . .

AMOS: For what?

DAVID: Well . . . maybe play some ball this summer.

AMOS [*glances at* PAT]: Who said I'm playing ball?

DAVID [*as carelessly as possible*]: What are you going to do with yourself?

AMOS: Pump your gas. . . . Bring you the money every night. Wait for something good to happen. [*A bitter little laugh.*] I mean the day they announced they're building the new main highway right past your gas station I knew *something* good had to happen to me. [*Laughing.*] I mean it just *had* to, Dave! [*Now with real feeling.*] Baby hasn't come yet? [DAVID *shakes his head, disturbed by his brother's bitterness.*] Overdue, ain't she? [*Takes a drag on his cigarette.*]

DAVID: A little.

AMOS: Well, if it's a boy . . . [*Glancing at* PAT *and defiantly blowing out smoke.*] Don't have him pitchin' down the cellar. *With a wink at* DAVID, *he goes out. After a moment* DAVID *goes to* PAT.

DAVID: Why must you go, Dad? Work with me here, I've plenty for everybody, I don't need it all.

PAT: Inhaling cigarettes in those glorious lungs. I couldn't bear to watch him destroying my work that way.

SHORY [*at the fireplace*]: Come on, Pat, pinochle.

DAVID [*beckoning* GUS *over to the right*]: Hey, Gus, I want to talk to you.

PAT [*going to* SHORY. *Without the old conviction*]: Fireplace heat is ruination to the arteries.

PAT *takes* GUS*'s place,* GUS *coming to the right.*

SHORY [*mixing the deck*]: So you'll drop dead warm. Sit down. [*He deals.*]

DAVID *and* GUS *are at right.* J.B. *continues sleeping. The card game begins.*

DAVID: I want you to do something for me, Gus. In a little more than thirty days I'll have four or five mink for every bitch in those cages. Four to one.

GUS: Well, don't count the chickens . . .

DAVID: No, about this I'm sure. I want to mortgage the shop. Before you answer . . . I'm not being an Indian giver. I signed sixty percent of the shop over to you because you're worth it—I didn't want what don't belong to me and I still don't. I just want you to sign so I can borrow some money on the shop. I need about twenty-five hundred dollars.

GUS: I can ask why?

DAVID: Sure. I want to buy some more breeders.

GUS: Oh. Well, why not use the money you have?

DAVID: Frankly, Gus . . . [*Laughs confidently.*] . . . I don't have any other money.

GUS: Ah, go on now, don't start kidding me . . .

DAVID: No, it's the truth. I've damn near as many mink out there as Dan Dibble. That costs big money. What do you say?

PAT *and* SHORY *look up now and listen while playing their hands.*

GUS [*thinks a moment*]: Why do you pick on the shop to mortgage? You could get twenty-five hundred on the gas station, or the quarry, or the farm . . . [*Slight pause.*]

DAVID: I did. I've got everything mortgaged. Everything but the shop.

GUS [*shocked*]: Dave, I can't believe this!

DAVID [*indicates out of the right window*]: Well, look at them out there. I've got a *ranch*. You didn't think I had enough cash to buy that many, did you?

GUS [*gets up trying to shake off his alarm*]: But, Dave, this is mink. Who knows what can happen to them? I don't understand how you can take everything you own and sink it in . . .

DAVID: Four for one, Gus. If prices stay up I can make sixty thousand dollars this year.

GUS: But how can you be sure; you can't . . .

DAVID: I'm sure.

GUS: But how can you be . . . ?

DAVID [*more nervously now, wanting to end this tack*]: I'm sure. Isn't it possible? To be sure?

GUS: Yes, but why? [*Pause.*] Why are you sure?

J.B. [*suddenly erupting on the couch*]: Good Good and . . . ! [*He sits up rubbing himself.*] What happened to those radiators you were going to put into this house? [*He gets up, goes to the fire, frozen.*] You could hang meat in this room.

DAVID [*to J.B.*]: You're always hanging meat.

GUS: I don't know how to answer you. I have worked very hard in the shop . . . I . . . [*His reasonableness breaks.*] You stand there and don't seem to realize you'll be wiped out if those mink go, and now you want more yet!

DAVID: *I said they're not going to die!*

J.B. [*to PAT and SHORY*]: Who's going to die? What're they talking about?

DAVID: Nothin'. [*He looks out of the window.* J.B. *watches him, mystified.*]

PAT: I think Amos would smoke a pipe instead of those cigarettes, if you told him, Shory.

J.B.: Dave, you want a baby carriage y'know.

DAVID [*half turns*]: Heh? . . . Yeh, sure.

J.B.: I figured you forgot to ask me so I ordered a baby carriage for you.

DAVID *turns back to the window as.* . . .

Matter of fact, it's in the store. [*With great enthusiasm.*] Pearl grey! Nice soft rubber tires too . . . boy, one thing I love to see . . .

DAVID [*turns to him, restraining*]: All right, will you stop talking?

J.B. *is shocked. In a moment he turns and goes to the rack,*
starts getting into his coat. DAVID *crosses quickly to him.*
    John, what the hell! [*He takes* J.B.*'s arm.*]

J.B.: You unnerve me, Dave! You unnerve me! A man acts a
    certain way when he's going to be a father, and by Jesus I
    want him to act that way.

SHORY: Another moviegoer! Why should he worry about some-
    thing he can't change?

DAVID: I've got a million things to think of, John. I want to ask
    you.

J.B.: What?

DAVID [*hangs* J.B.*'s coat up*]: I want to get a buy on a new
    Buick; maybe you can help me swindle that dealer you know
    in Burley. I'm taking Hester to California in about a month.
    Sit down.

J.B. [*suddenly pointing at him*]: That's what unnerves me! You
    don't seem to realize what's happening. You can't take a
    month-old baby in a car to California.

DAVID [*a blank, shocked look*]: Well, I meant . . .

J.B. [*laughs, slaps his back relieved at this obvious truth*]: The
    trouble with you is, you don't realize that she didn't swell up
    because she swallowed an olive! [GUS *and he laugh;* DAVID
    tries to.] You're a poppa, boy! You're the guy he's going to
    call Pop!
        There is a commotion of footsteps upstairs. DAVID *goes*
    quickly to the landing. BELLE *hurries down. She is sniffling,*
    sobbing.

DAVID: What happened?
        BELLE *touches his shoulder kindly but brushes right past*
    him to the fireplace where she picks up a wood basket.
        [DAVID *continues going to her.*] What happened, Belle!

BELLE [*standing with the wood*]: She's having it, she's having
    it. [*She hurries to the landing,* DAVID *behind her.*]

DAVID: What does the doctor say? Belle! How is she? [*He*
    catches her arm.]

BELLE: I don't know. She shouldn't have fallen that time. She
    shouldn't have fallen, Davey. Oh dear . . .
        She bursts into a sob and rushes upstairs. DAVID *stands gap-*

ing upward. But GUS *is staring at* DAVID. *After a long moment . . .*

GUS [*quietly*]: Hester fell down?

DAVID [*turns slowly to him after an instant of his own*]: What?

GUS: Hester had a fall?

DAVID: Yeh, some time ago.

GUS: You had her to the doctor?

DAVID: Yeh.

GUS: He told you the baby would be possibly dead? [*Pause.*]

DAVID: What're you talking about?

GUS [*quavering*]: I think you know what I'm talking about.

DAVID *is speechless. Walks to a chair and sits on the arm as though, at the price of terrible awkwardness, to simulate ease. Always glancing at* GUS, *he gets up unaccountably, and in a broken, uncontrolled voice . . .*

DAVID: What are you talking about?

GUS: I understand why you were so sure about the mink. But I sign no mortgage on the shop. I do not bet on dead children.

DAVID *is horrified at the revelation. He stands rigidly, his fists clenched. He might sit down or spring at* GUS *or weep.*

J.B.: He couldn't think a thing like that. He . . .

He looks to DAVID *for reinforcement, but* DAVID *is standing there hurt and silent and self-horrified.* J.B. *goes to* DAVID.

Dave, you wouldn't want a thing like that. [*He shakes him.*] Dave!

DAVID [*glaring at* GUS]: I'd cut my throat!

He walks downstage from J.B., *looking at* GUS. *His movements are wayward, restless, like one caught in a strange cul-de-sac.* GUS *is silent.*

Why do you look at me that way? [*Glances at* J.B. *then slowly back to* GUS.] Why do you look that way? I'm only telling you what happened. A person has to look at facts, doesn't he? I heard something at the door and I opened it . . . and there she was lying on the step. A fact is a fact, isn't it? [*They don't reply. Bursting out.*] Well, for Jesus' sake, if you . . . !

GUS [*a shout*]: What fact! She fell! So the baby is dead because she fell! Is this a fact?!!

DAVID [*moves away from* GUS's *direction, in high tension*]: I didn't say dead. It doesn't have to be dead to be . . . to . . . [*Breaks off.*]

GUS: To be what?

Pause.

DAVID: To be a curse on us. It can come wrong . . . A fall can make them that way. The doctor told me. [GUS *looks unconvinced.*] The trouble with you is that you think I got a special angel watching over me.

SHORY [*pointing at Gus*]: He said it that time, brother!

GUS [*to* SHORY *too*]: A man needs a special angel to have a live child?

DAVID [*furiously*]: Who said he was going to be dead?!

GUS: What are you excited about? [*Takes his arm.*] Take it easy, sit . . .

DAVID [*freeing his aim*]: Stop humoring me, will you? Dan Dibble'll have my new mink here tonight. I got all the papers ready . . . [*Goes to a drawer, takes out papers.*] All you do is sign and . . .

GUS [*suddenly he rushes to David, pulls the papers out of his hand, throws them down*]: Are you mad! [*He frightens* DAVID *into immobility.*] There is no catastrophe upstairs, there is no guarantee up there for your mink. [*He grasps* DAVID's *arm, pleadingly.*] Dave . . .

DAVID: If you say that again I'm going to throw you out of this house!

J.B. [*nervously*]: Oh, come on now, come on now.

From above a scream of pain is heard. DAVID *freezes.* GUS *looks up.*

GUS [*to* DAVID]: Don't say that again.

DAVID *thrusts his hands into his pockets as though they might reveal him too. Under great tension he attempts to speak reasonably. His voice leaps occasionally, he clears his throat.* GUS *never takes his eyes off him.* DAVID *walks from* J.B. *unwillingly.*

DAVID: I'm a lucky man, John. Everything I've ever gotten came . . . straight out of the blue. There's nothing mad about it. It's facts. When I couldn't have Hester unless Old Man

Falk got out of the way, he was killed just like it was specially for me. When I couldn't fix the Marmon . . . a man walks in from the middle of the night . . . and fixes it for me. I buy a lousy little gas station . . . they build a highway in front of it. That's lucky. You pay for that.

SHORY: Damn right you do.

GUS: Where is such a law?

DAVID: I don't know. [*Observes a silence. He walks to the windows.*] Of all the people I've heard of I'm the only one who's never paid. Well . . . I think the holiday's over. [*Turns toward upstairs, with great sorrow.*] I think we're about due to join up with the rest of you. I'll have almost sixty thousand dollars when I market my mink . . . but it won't be money I got without paying for it. And that's why I put everything in them. That's why I'm sure. Because from here on in we're paid for. I saw it in black and white when she fell. [*With a heartbroken tone.*] God help me, we're paid for now. I'm not afraid of my luck anymore, and I'm going to play it for everything it's worth.

GUS: David, you break my heart. This is from Europe this idea. This is from Asia, from the rotten places, not America.

DAVID: No?

GUS: Here you are not a worm, a louse in the earth; here you are a man. A man deserves everything here!

SHORY: Since when?

GUS [*strongly to* SHORY]: Since forever!

SHORY: Then I must have been born before that.

GUS [*angrily now*]: I beg your pardon, he is not you and do me a favor and stop trying to make him like you.

DAVID: He's not making me anything.

GUS: He won't be happy until he does, I can tell you! [*Indicating* SHORY.] This kind of people never are.

SHORY: What kind of people?

GUS: Your kind! *His* life he can make golden, if he wants.

SHORY: Unless the walls blow out.

GUS: If he don't go chasing after whores his walls won't blow out. [*Quietly.*] And I beg your pardon. I didn't mean nothing personal.

J.B. [*goes to* DAVID]: I'll lend you the money for the mink, Dave.

GUS: Are you mad?

J.B.: I can see what he means, Gus. [*Looks at* DAVID.] It takes a great kind of man to prepare himself that way. A man does have to pay. It's just the way it happens, senseless.

[*He glances upstairs, then to* DAVID.]

It's true. It always happens senseless.

J.B.: I'll back you, Dave.

DAVID: I'd like to pay him tonight if I can . . .

They all turn to look up as BELLE *appears, slowly descending the stairs. They do not hear her until she is a little way down. Her usual expression of wide-eyed bewilderment is on her face, but now she is tense, and descends looking at* DAVID. *She half sniffs, half sobs into her kerchief. She stops on the stairs.* DAVID *rises. She half laughs, half snivels in a quiet ecstasy of excitement, and weakly motions him upstairs. He comes toward her questioningly, to the landing.*

BELLE: Go . . . Go up.

DAVID: What. What . . . ?

BELLE [*suddenly bursts out and rushes down and flings her arms about him*]: Oh, Davey, Davey.

DAVID [*ripping her free, he roars in her face*]: What happened?! [*With a sob of grief in his voice, he grips her.*] Belle! *The cry of a baby is suddenly heard from above. The sound almost throws* DAVID *back, away from the stairs. He stands stock still, hard as a rock, looking upward, his mouth fallen open.*

BELLE [*still half-sobbing*]: It's a boy. A perfect baby boy! *She now breaks info full sobs and rushes up the stairs. Everything is still a moment,* DAVID *stares at nothing. The cry sounds again. He looks upward again as though to let it sink in.* J.B. *goes to him, hand extended.*

J.B. [*filled with joy, and gravely*]: Dave.

DAVID *dumbly shakes his hand, a weak smile on his face.*

A boy, a boy, Dave! Just what you wanted!

A strange short laugh leaps from DAVID. *An easier but still tense laugh comes.* PAT *goes to him and shakes his hand.*

PAT: Dave, a new generation!

GUS [*smilingly*]: Well? You see? [*Laughs.*] A good man gets what a good man makes. [*Hits* DAVID *jovially.*] Wake up now! Good luck!

Gus tosses a quarter to SHORY.

GUS: It's the first time you've been right since I knew you.

J.B.: Come out of the ether. Take a look at him, Dave.

DAVID *rushes out. They stand astonished for a moment.*
What do you suppose come over him?

GUS: What else could come over him? . . . he's ashamed.

GUS *hurries out the door. The others remain in silence. Then one by one they look upstairs toward the sound of the baby's crying.*
Slow Curtain.

Scene ii

Before the curtain rises thunder is heard.

It is one month later. The living room. Night.

The room is empty and in darkness. A bolt of lightning illuminates it through the windows, then darkness again. Now the door to the outside opens and HESTER *enters. She is very tense but her motions are minute, as though she were mentally absorbed and had entirely forgotten her surroundings. Without removing her coat or galoshes she comes to the center of the room and stands there staring. Then she goes to a window and looks out. A flash of lightning makes her back a step from the window; and without further hesitation she goes to the phone, switching on a nearby light.*

HESTER [*she watches the window as she waits*]: Hello? Gus? Where have you been, I've been ringing you for an hour. [*She listens.*] Well, look, could you come over here? Right now, I mean. It would *not* be interfering, Gus, I want to talk to you. He's outside. Gus, you've got to come here—his mink are going to die. [*She keeps glancing at the window.*] He doesn't know it yet, but he'll probably see it any minute. Dan Dibble called before. . . . He's lost over thirty of his already. . . . They use the same fish. . . . I want you here when he notices. [*She turns suddenly toward the door.*] He's coming in. You hurry over now. . . . Please!

She hangs up, and starts for the door, but as though to compose herself she stops, and starts toward a chair when she realizes she still has her coat and galoshes on. She is kicking off the galoshes when DAVID *enters. He looks up at her, and with a slight glance upstairs . . .*

DAVID: Everything all right?

HESTER: Why?

DAVID: I thought I heard a call or a scream.

HESTER: No, there was no scream.

DAVID: I guess it was the lightning. Is he all right? [*Of the baby.*]

HESTER: There's no gate there, you can go up and see.

DAVID: How can I go to him with my hands so bloody? [*She turns from him. He starts for the door.*]

HESTER: I thought you were through feeding.

DAVID: I am. I'm just grinding some for tomorrow.

HESTER: Are they all right?

DAVID: I never saw them so strung up. I think it's the hail banging on the cages. [*There is a momentary hiatus as he silently asks for leave to go.*] I just wondered if he was all right. [*He takes a step.*]

HESTER [*suddenly*]: Don't go out again, Davey. Please. You told me yourself, they ought to be left alone when they're whelping.

DAVID: I've got to be there, Hess, I've just got to. I . . . [*He goes to her.*] I promise you, after they whelp we'll go away, we'll travel . . . I'm going to make a queen's life for you.

HESTER: Don't go out.

DAVID: I'll be in right away . . .

HESTER [*grasps his arms*]: I don't want them to be so important, Davey!

DAVID: But everything we've got is in them. You know that.

HESTER: I'm not afraid of being poor . . .

DAVID: That's 'cause you never were—and you'll never be. You're going to have a life like a . . .

HESTER: Why do you keep saying that? I don't want it, I don't need it! I don't care what happens out there! And I don't want you to care. Do you hear what I say, I don't want you to care!

A bolt of lightning floods suddenly through the windows. DAVID starts. Then hurries to the door.

HESTER [*frightened now*]: Davey! [DAVID *stops, does not turn.*] You can't stop the lightning, can you? [*He does not turn still. She goes closer to him, pleading.*] I know how hard you worked, but it won't be the first year's work that ever went for nothing in the world. It happens that way, doesn't it?

DAVID [*he turns to her slowly. Now his emotions seem to flood him*]: Not when a man doesn't make any mistakes. I kept them alive all year. Not even one got sick. I didn't make a mistake. And now this storm comes, just when I need it calm, just tonight . . .

HESTER: You talk as though the sun were shining everywhere else but here, as though the sky is making thunder just to knock you down.

DAVID [*he looks at her long as though she had reached into him*]: Yeh, that's the way I talk. [*He seems about to sob.*] Bear with me, Hess—only a little while. [*He moves to go.*]

HESTER: Davey . . . the house is grey. Like the old paint was creeping back on the walls. When will we sit and talk again? When will you pick up the baby . . . ?

DAVID [*comes alive*]: I did, Hess . . .

HESTER: You never did. And why is that?

DAVID: When you were out of the house . . .

HESTER: Never, not since he's been born. Can't you tell me why? [DAVID *turns and opens the door. Her fear raises her voice.*] Can't you tell me why? [*He starts out.*] Davey, tell me why! [*He goes out. She calls out the door*] Davey, I don't understand! Come back here!

In a moment, she comes away, closing the door. Her hands are lightly clasped to her throat. She comes to a halt in the room; now she turns on a lamp. She suddenly hears some-

thing behind her, turns, and takes a step toward the door as
GUS *quietly enters.*

HESTER [*relieved*]: Oh, Gus!

GUS [*glancing toward the door*]: Is he coming right back?

HESTER: He goes in and out, I don't know. You'll stay here tonight, won't you?

GUS: The first thing to do is sit down.

As he leads her to the couch—she is near tears.

HESTER: I kept calling you and calling you.

GUS [*taking off his coat*]: Now get hold of yourself; there's nothing to do till he finds out. I'm sorry, I was in Burley all afternoon, I just got home. What did Dibble tell you? [*He returns to her.*]

HESTER: Just that he was losing animals, and he thought it was silkworm in the feed. They share the same carload.

GUS: Ah. David notices nothing? [*A gesture toward outside with his head.*]

HESTER: He just says they're strung up, but that's the lightning. It takes time for them to digest.

GUS: Well then, we'll wait and see. [*He goes to the window, looks out.*] This storm is going to wipe out the bridges. It's terrible.

HESTER: What am I going to do, Gus? He worked all year on those animals.

GUS: We will do what we have to, Hester, that's what we will do. [*He turns to her, taking out an envelope.*] Actually, I was coming over tonight anyway . . . To say goodbye.

HESTER: Goodbye!

GUS: In here I explain. [*He places the envelope on the mantel.*] When I am gone, give it to him. I can't argue with him no more.

HESTER: You mean you're moving away?

GUS: I am going to Chicago. There is an excellent position for me. Double what I can make here.

HESTER: But why are you going?

GUS: I told you, I can make double . . .

HESTER [*gets up*]: Don't treat me like a baby, why are you going? [*Slight pause.*]

GUS: Well . . . Actually, I am lonely. [*Laughs slightly.*] There is plenty of girls here, but no wifes, Hester. Thirty-seven years is a long time for a man to wash his own underwear.

HESTER [*touched*]: You and your red-headed girls!

GUS: I was always a romantic man. You know that, don't you? Truly.

HESTER: But to give up a business and go traipsing off just for . . . ?

GUS: Why not? What made me give up Detroit to come here?

HESTER: Really, Gus?

GUS: Certainly. Moving is very necessary for me. [*Pause.*] I'm leaving tomorrow night.

HESTER: But why? I suppose I should understand, but I can't. [*Pause.* GUS *looks directly at her.*] It doesn't make sense. [*Insistently.*] Gus?

GUS: [*pause. For a long time he keeps her in his eye*]: Because I have no courage to stay here. [*Pause.*] I was talking today with a doctor in Burley. I believe David . . . is possibly losing his mind.

She does not react. She stands there gaping at him. He waits. With no sound she backs a few steps, then comes downstage and lightly sets both hands on the couch, never taking her eyes from him. A pause. As though hearing what he said again, she is impelled to move again, to a chair on whose back she sets a hand—facing him now. They stand so a moment.

I thought surely you knew. Or at least you would know soon. [*She does not answer.*] Do you know?

HESTER: I've almost thought so sometimes. . . . But I can't believe he . . .

GUS [*a new directness, now that she has taken the blow*]: I have been trying to straighten him out all month. But I have no more wisdom, Hester. I . . . I would like to take him to the doctors in Burley.

HESTER [*shocked*]: Burley!

GUS: Tonight. They will know what to say to him there.

HESTER [*horrified*]: No, he's not going there.

GUS: It is no disgrace. You are talking like a silly woman.

HESTER: He's not going there! There's nothing wrong with him. He's worried, that's all . . .

GUS: When those animals begin dying he will be more than worried. Nothing worse could possibly happen . . .

HESTER: No. If he can take the shock tonight he'll be all right. I think it's better if they die.

GUS: For God's sake, no!

HESTER: All his life he's been waiting for it. All his life, waiting, waiting for something to happen. It'll be over now, all over, don't you see? Just stay here tonight. And when it happens, you'll talk to him . . .

GUS: What he has lost I can't put back, Hester. He is not a piece of machinery.

HESTER [stops moving]: What has he lost? What do you mean, lost?

GUS: What a man must have, what a man must believe. That on this earth he is the boss of his life. Not the leafs in the teacups, not the stars. In Europe I seen already millions of Davids walking around, millions. They gave up already to know that they are the boss. They gave up to know that they deserve this world. And now here too, with such good land, with such a . . . such a big sky they are saying . . . I hear it every day . . . that it is somehow unnatural for a man to have a sweet life and nice things. Daily they wait for catastrophe. A man must understand the presence of God in his hands. And when he don't understand it he is trapped. David is trapped, Hester. You understand why everything he has is in the mink?

HESTER [wide-eyed]: It's the baby, isn't it. He thought it was going to be . . .

GUS: Dead, yes. Say, say out now. I was here that night. He always wanted so much to have a son and that is why he saw him dead. This, what he wanted most of all he couldn't have. This finally would be his catastrophe. And then everything would be guaranteed for him. And that is why he put everything in those animals.

HESTER: Gus . . .

GUS: The healthy baby stole from David his catastrophe, Hester. Perfect he was born and David was left with every penny he owns in an animal that can die like this . . . [*Snaps his fingers.*] and the catastrophe still on its way.

HESTER [*seeing the reason*]: He never touched the baby . . .

GUS: How can he touch him? He is bleeding with shame, Hester. Because he betrayed his son, and he betrayed you. And now if those animals die he will look into the tea leafs of his mind, into the sky he will look where he always looked, and if he sees retribution there . . . you will not call him worried any more. Let me take him to Burley before he notices anything wrong in the cages.

HESTER: No. He's Davey, he's not some . . .

GUS: They will know what to do there!

HESTER: I know what to do! [*She moves away and faces him.*] I could have warned him. . . . Dan called before he started feeding.

GUS [*shocked and furious*]: Hester!

HESTER: I wanted them dead! I want them dead now, those beautiful rats!

GUS: How could you do that!

HESTER: He's got to lose. Once and for all he's got to lose. I always knew it had to happen, let it happen now, before the baby can see and understand. You're not taking him anywhere. He'll be happy again. It'll be over and he'll be happy!

GUS [*unwillingly*]: Hester.

HESTER: No, I'm not afraid now. It'll be over now.

GUS: What will be over, Hester? He took out last week an insurance policy. A big one. [HESTER *stops moving.*] It covers his life.

HESTER: No, Gus.

GUS: What will be over?

HESTER [*a cry*]: No, Gus! [*Breaks into sobbing.*]

GUS [*taking her by the arms*]: Get hold now, get hold!

HESTER [*sobbing, shaking her head negatively*]: Davey, Davey . . . he was always so fine, what happened to him . . . !

GUS: He mustn't see you this way . . . ! Nothing is worse than . . .

HESTER [*trying to break from* GUS *to go out*]: Davey, Davey . . . !

GUS: Stop it, Hester! He's shamed enough!

He has her face in his hands as the door suddenly opens and DAVID *is standing there.* GUS *releases her. They stand apart.* DAVID *has stopped moving in surprise. He looks at her, then at* GUS, *then at her.* DAVID *goes toward her.*

DAVID [*astonished, alarmed*]: Hess. What's the matter?

HESTER: Nothing . . . How is everything outside?

DAVID: It's still hailing . . . [*Stops. With an edge of self-accusation.*] Why were you crying?

HESTER [*her voice still wet*]: I wasn't really.

DAVID [*feeling the awkwardness, glances at both; to* GUS]: Why were you holding her?

HESTER [*with an attempt at a laugh*]: He wasn't holding me. He's decided to go to Chicago and . . .

DAVID [*mystified, to* GUS]: Chicago! Why . . . ?

HESTER [*tries to laugh*]: He wants to find a wife! Imagine?

DAVID [*to* GUS]: All of a sudden you . . . ?

HESTER [*unbuttoning his coat, ready to weep and trying to be gay*]: Let's have some tea and sit up till way late and talk! Don't go out anymore, Davey. . . . From now on I'm not letting you out of my sight. . . . There are so many nice things to talk about!

She has his coat and has just stepped away with a gross animation.

DAVID [*deeply worried. Brushing her attempt away*]: Why were you crying, Hester?

The phone rings. HESTER *fairly leaps at the sound. She starts quickly for the phone but* DAVID *is close to it and picks it up easily, slightly puzzled at her frantic eagerness to take it.*

HESTER: It's probably Ellie. I promised to lend her a hat for tomorrow.

DAVID [*looks at her perplexed. He lifts the receiver*]: Yes?

As she speaks HESTER *steps away from him, in fear now.* GUS *changes position instinctively, almost as though for physical advantage.*

Mr. Dibble? No, he isn't here; I don't expect him. Oh! Well, he isn't here yet. What's it all about? [*Listens.*] What

are you talking about; have I got what under control? [*Listens. Now with horror.*] Of course I've fed! Why didn't you call me, you know I feed before this! God damn your soul, you know I use the same feed he does! [*Roars.*] Don't tell me he called me! Don't . . . ! [*Listens*] When did he call?
Breaks off; listens. He turns, listening, to HESTER; *slowly, an expression of horrified perplexity and astonishment grips his face. His eyes stay on* HESTER.

Well, they seem all right now . . . maybe it hasn't had time to grip them. [*Still into the phone.*] Yeh . . . yeh . . . all right, I'll wait for him.
He hangs up weakly. For a long time he looks at her. Then he looks at GUS *and back to her as though connecting them somehow.*

What . . . Why . . . didn't you tell me he called?

HESTER [*suddenly she dares not be too near him; she holds out a hand to touch and ward him off . . . she is a distance from him*]: Davey . . .

DAVID: Why didn't you stop me from feeding?

GUS: Dan'll be here. Maybe he can do something.

DAVID [*facing* HESTER]: What can he do? Something's wrong in the feed! He can't pull it out of their stomachs! [*With welling grief. To* HESTER.] Why didn't you tell me? [HESTER *retreats a few inches.*] Why are you moving away from me? [*He suddenly reaches out and catches her arm.*] You wanted them to die!

HESTER [*straining at his grip*]: You always said something had to happen. It's better this way, isn't it?

DAVID: Better?! My boy is a pauper, we're on the bottom of a hole, how is it better!

HESTER [*her fear alone makes her brave*]: Then I . . . I think I'll have to go away, Davey. I can't stay here, then.
She moves toward the stairs. He lets her move a few steps, then moves across to her and she stops and faces him.

DAVID: You can't . . . What did you say?

HESTER: I can't live with you, Davey. Not with the baby.

DAVID: No, Hester . . .

HESTER: I don't want him to see you this way. It's a harmful thing. I'm going away.

DAVID [*he breathes as though about to burst into weeping. He looks to* GUS, *stares at him, then back to her. Incredibly*]: You're going with him?

HESTER [*she darts a suddenly frightened glance toward* GUS]: Oh, no, no, I didn't mean that. He was going anyway.

DAVID [*it is truer to him now*]: You're going with him.

HESTER: No, David, I'm not going with anybody . . .

DAVID [*with certainty. Anger suddenly stalks him*]: You're going with him!

HESTER: No, Davey . . . !

DAVID [*To* GUS]: You told her not to tell me!

HESTER: He wasn't even here when Dan phoned!

DAVID: How do I know where he was! [*To Gus*] You think I'm a blind boy?!

HESTER: You're talking like a fool!

DAVID: You couldn't have done this to me! He wants you!
He starts to stride for GUS. HESTER *gets in front of him.*

HESTER: I did it! [*Grabs his coat.*] Davey, I did it myself!

DAVID: No, you couldn't have! Not you! [*To* GUS.] You think I've fallen apart? You want her . . . ?
He starts to push her aside, knocking a chair over, going for GUS. *She slaps him hard across the face. He stops moving.*

HESTER [*with loathing and heartbreak*]: I did it!
For an instant they are still, she watching for his reaction. He quietly draws in a sob, looking at her in grief.

HESTER: I wanted you like you were, Davey—a good man, able to do anything. You were always a good man, why can't you understand that?

DAVID: A good man! You pick up a phone and everything you've got dies in the ground! A man! What good is a man!

HESTER: You can start again, start fresh and clean!

DAVID: For what! For what!! The world is a madhouse, what can you build in a madhouse that won't be knocked down when you turn your back!

HESTER: It was you made it all and you destroyed it! I'm going,

Davey . . . [*With a sob.*] I can't bear any more. [*She rushes to the landing.*]

DAVID [*A call, and yet strangled by sobs*]: Hester . . .

HESTER *halts, looks at him. His hands raised toward her, shaken and weeping, he moves toward the landing . . . frantically.*

I love you . . . I love you. . . . Don't . . . don't . . . don't.
He reaches her, and sobbing, lost, starts drawing her down to him as the door, left, swings open. DAN DIBBLE *rushes in and halts when he sees* DAVID. *He carries a small satchel.*

DIBBLE [*indicating downstage, right*]: I've been out there looking for you, what are you doing in here? I've got something may help them. Come on. [*He starts for the door.*]

DAVID: I don't want to look at them, Dan. [*He goes to a chair.*]

DIBBLE: You can't be sure, it might take . . . [*Opens the door.*]

DAVID: No, I'm sure they digested, it's over two hours.

DIBBLE [*stops moving suddenly at door*]: Over two hours what?

DAVID: Since I fed them.

DIBBLE: You didn't give them this morning's load of fish?

DAVID: What else could I give them? The load I split with you, goddamit.

DIBBLE: Well, you just couldn't't've, David. They don't show a sign yet: that kind of silkworm'll kill them in twenty minutes. You must've . . .

DAVID: Silkworm.—But my fish wasn't wormy . . .

DIBBLE: They don't look like worms, they're very small, you wouldn't have noticed them, they're black, about the size of a . . .

DAVID: Poppyseed . . .

DIBBLE: A grain of ground pepper, yah. Come on . . . [*But* DAVID *is motionless, staring . . .*] Well? You want me to look at them?

DAVID *slowly sits in a chair.*

GUS: At least have a look, Dave. [*Slight pause.*]

DAVID [*wondrously; but also an edge of apology*]: . . . I saw them, Dan. I didn't know what they were but I decided not to take any chances, so I threw them away.

DIBBLE [*angering*]: But you couldn't have gone over every piece of fish!

DAVID: Well I . . . yah, I did, Dan. Most of it was okay, but the ones with the black specks I threw away.

HESTER: Davey!—you saved them!

DAVID: Well, you told me to watch the feed very carefully, Dan—I figured you'd notice them the same as me!

DIBBLE: But you know nobody's got the time to go over every goddam piece of fish!

DAVID: But I thought everybody did!—I swear, Dan!

DIBBLE: God Almighty, Dave, a man'd think you'd warn him if you saw silkworm!—the least you could've done is call me.

DAVID: I started to, I had the phone in my hand—but it seemed ridiculous, me telling you something. Listen, let me give you some of my breeders to start you off again.

DIBBLE: No—no . . .

DAVID: Please, Dan, go out and pick whatever you like.

DIBBLE: . . . Well, I might think about that, but I'm too old to start all over again, I don't think I could get up the steam. Well, goodnight.

DIBBLE *exits.*

GUS *and* HESTER *stand watching* DAVID *who is puzzled and astonished.*

DAVID: I can't believe it. He's the best in the business.

GUS: Not anymore.

HESTER: This wasn't something from the sky, dear. This was you only. You must see that now, don't you?

The baby crying is heard from above.

I'd better go up, he's hungry. Come up?—Why don't you, Dave?

DAVID [*awkwardly*]: I will . . . right away. [HESTER *exits. His face is rapt.*] But they couldn't all have made their own luck!—J.B. with his drinking, Shory with his whores, Dad and Amos . . . and you losing your shop. [*Seizing on it.*] And I could never have fixed that Marmon if you hadn't walked in like some kind of an angel!—that Marmon wasn't me!

GUS: You'd have towed it to Newton and fixed it there without me. [*Grasps* DAVID's *hand.*] But is that really the question anyway? Of course bad things must happen. And you can't help it when God drops the other shoe. But whether you lay there or get up again—that's the part that's entirely up to you, that's for sure.

DAVID: You don't understand it either, do you.

GUS: No, but I live with it. All I know is you are a good man, but also you have luck. So you have to grin and bear it—you are lucky!

DAVID: For now.

GUS: Well, listen—"for now" is a very big piece of "forever."

HESTER [*from above*]: Dave? You coming up?

GUS: Go on, kiss the little fellow.

DAVID: . . . I had the phone in my hand to call him. And I put it down. I had his whole ranch right here in my hand.

GUS: You mean you were a little bit like God . . . for him.

DAVID: Yes. Except I didn't know it.

GUS [*a thumb pointing heavenward*]: Maybe he doesn't know either.

HESTER [*from above*]: David? Are you there?

GUS: Goodnight, Dave.

DAVID [*with a farewell wave to* GUS, *calls upstairs*]: Yes, I'm here!

He goes to the stairs. A shock of thunder strikes. He quickly turns toward the windows, the old apprehension in his face.
      . . . [*To himself.*] For now.
[*With a self-energized determination in his voice and body.*] Comin' up!
As he mounts the stairs a rumble of thunder sounds in the distance.

Available in Penguin Classics editions:

All My Sons
Told against the setting of a suburban backyard in the 1940s, Miller's play is a classic American drama about the idealization of a father, the loss of a son, and the secrets that destroy a family. Winner of the Drama Critics Circle Award for Best New Play in 1947, *All My Sons* was the work that established Arthur Miller as the new voice in the American theater. ISBN 0-14-118546-5

The Crucible
"I believe the reader will discover here the essential nature of one of the strangest and most awful chapters in human history," Arthur Miller wrote in an introduction to *The Crucible*, his classic play about the witch-hunts and trials in seventeenth-century Salem, Massachusetts. Based on historical people and actual events, Miller's drama is a thinly veiled indictment of the McCarthy trials of the early 1950s. ISBN 0-14-243733-6

Death of a Salesman
All his life Willy Loman has been a traveling salesman who made a decent living—but not more. Dreams and evasions have kept him from seeing himself as he is. He has learned the American go-getter philosophy by heart, and passed it on to his sons, to their undoing. And then, at sixty-three, finally forced to face reality, Willy turns away, down the only road open to him. Out of this simple human situation, Arthur Miller has fashioned the winner of the Pulitzer Prize and Drama Critics Circle Award in 1949 and one of the greatest dramas of our time.
ISBN 0-14-118097-8

All of the above include an introduction by Christopher Bigsby

Available in Penguin Plays editions

After the Fall
Arthur Miller has set this devastating play inside a mind. The mind belongs to Quentin, a lawyer with a lofty reputation and a prosecutor's zeal for pursuing the finest threads of guilt. Yet the guilt that most obsesses Quentin is his own: his guilt as a son and husband, friend, lover, and man. And in the course of his plunge through the labyrinths of consciousness and conscience, Quentin will be joined by several hostile witnesses—from the partner he abandoned to the beautiful, childlike wife he couldn't save. Masterly in its orchestration, searing in its candor, *After the Fall* is a victory of the moral imagination. ISBN 0-14-048162-1

A View from the Bridge
Longshoreman Eddie Carbone struggles with his predictable life, the arrival of two of his wife's relatives from Italy, and his true feelings for his niece Catherine.
ISBN 0-14-048135-4

Also available from Arthur Miller in Penguin Plays editions

Broken Glass	ISBN 0-14-024938-9
The Crucible	ISBN 0-14-048138-9
Death of a Salesman	ISBN 0-14-048134-6
An Enemy of the People	ISBN 0-14-048140-0
Incident at Vichy	ISBN 0-14-048193-1
Mr. Peters' Connections	ISBN 0-14-048245-8
The Price	ISBN 0-14-048194-X
The Ride Down Mt. Morgan	ISBN 0-14-048244-X

Also by Arthur Miller:

Timebends
A Life
With passion, wit, and candor, Arthur Miller recalls his childhood in Harlem and Brooklyn during the 1920s and the Depression; his successes and failures in the theater and in Hollywood; the formation of his political beliefs that, two decades later, brought him into confrontation with the House Committee on Un-American Activities; and his later work on behalf of human rights as the president of PEN International. He writes with astonishing perception and tenderness of Marilyn Monroe, his second wife, as well as the host of famous and infamous that he has intersected with during his adventurous life. *Timebends* is Miller's love letter to the twentieth century: its energy, its humor, its chaos and moral struggles.

ISBN 0-14-024917-6

Echoes Down the Corridor
Collected Essays: 1944–2000
"A fascinating collection that reminds us that Miller's chief concern and great subject has always been the citizen in his world."—*Los Angeles Times*
Witty and wise, rich in artistry and insight, *Echoes Down the Corridor* gathers together a dazzling array of more than forty previously uncollected essays and works of reportage, reaffirming Arthur Miller's standing as one of the greatest writers of our time.

ISBN 0-14-200005-1

Homely Girl, A Life and Other Stories
This is a stunning collection of brilliant short fiction from the Pulitzer Prize–winning dramatist and one of the twentieth century's greatest writers. All three prose works in *Homely Girl, A Life* demonstrate all the insight, precision, and greatness of spirit of Miller's classic plays.

ISBN 0-14-025279-7

CLICK ON A CLASSIC
www.penguinclassics.com

The world's greatest literature at your fingertips

Constantly updated information on more than a thousand titles,
from Icelandic sagas to ancient Indian epics, Russian drama to
Italian romance, American greats to African masterpieces

•

The latest news on recent additions to the list, updated
editions, and specially commissioned translations

•

Original essays by leading writers

•

A wealth of background material, including biographies
of every classic author from Aristotle to Zamyatin, plot
synopses, readers' and teachers' guides, useful web links

•

Online desk and examination copy assistance for academics

•

Trivia quizzes, competitions, giveaways, news on
forthcoming screen adaptations